P9-EFG-618

AARON BURR

Hero or villain, patriot or traitor, Aaron Burr was many things to many men and women. A leading hero of the Revolution who became Vice-President of the United States, he then plotted against his country in an effort to carve an empire of his own in the West. In this incisive biography author William Wise unfolds a story of cross and double cross. Burr, who killed Alexander Hamilton in a duel, was called unprincipled, shrewd, conniving. Yet he was blissfully loyal to Thomas Jefferson—who repaid him by conspiring to break him politically. The exciting story of Aaron Burr is, in many respects, the story of the United States in its first decades.

LIVES TO

REMEMBER

AARON BURR

by William Wise

G. P. PUTNAM'S SONS  NEW YORK

92-Biog
Bur

Library of Congress Catalog Card Number: 68-15086

PRINTED IN THE UNITED STATES OF AMERICA
12216

To Nina and Alfred

Contents

AARON BURR

1.

"He Is Very Resolute"

O N MAY 4, 1812, a small transatlantic sailing ship, the *Aurora*, glided silently into Boston harbor and tied up at one of the city's wharves. Aboard was a most unusual passenger. He was a short, spare, middle-aged man with brilliant black eyes, who was traveling under an assumed name. On his passport, and on the ship's official records, he was listed as "Mr. Adolphus Arnot."

None of "Mr. Arnot's" fellow passengers had recognized him during the five weeks' voyage from England. He had taken every precaution to see that they did not; he had grown a beard to conceal his chin and had worn a black, ill-fitting wig to complete his disguise. Much of the time he had remained below in his cabin. Only Captain Potter of the *Aurora* knew that "Mr. Arnot" was really one of the most famous—and infamous—Americans of the age, that he was, in fact, the celebrated and notorious Colonel Aaron Burr.

When the *Aurora* docked that May afternoon in Boston, Burr was a ruined man. For several years he had chosen to remain in European exile; on his return he scarcely had a penny left to his name. His once-elegant suit was threadbare now; his overcoat had been left behind in England, where he had been forced to pawn it to raise money for his passage home. Yet, at one time, Burr had possessed considerable wealth and great political power. Only a single step—and a very short one—had stood between him and the Presidency of the United States.

Few leaders in America ever have risen as high, or fallen as swiftly, as Aaron Burr. Few have commanded so fanatically loyal a band of friends, or have been pursued by so implacable and remorseless an army of enemies. And few men who ever dwelled long in the public eye have left behind so many unanswered questions about themselves and their deeds as the proud, the secretive, and the always inscrutable Colonel Burr.

About seventy years before the *Aurora* arrived in Boston harbor, Aaron Burr's father—the Reverend Aaron Burr—left his New England home and traveled south to the colony of New Jersey. There he settled in Newark, and began to serve as minister of the First Presbyterian Church. He was an eloquent preacher and soon gained the esteem of his parishioners. But he was also an able classical scholar, and as time went by, he took more pleasure in teaching Latin, Greek and the Scriptures to the boys in the parish than he did in delivering sermons from the pulpit. In 1746, when he was just over thirty, he helped found the College of

New Jersey—now Princeton University—and before the year was out he had been named its president.

The Reverend Burr proved an excellent teacher and administrator. He knew instinctively how to arouse the enthusiasm of young students, and under his guidance the college in Newark became a great success. Within five years its enrollment had grown from eight to sixty and, in addition, there were forty younger boys attending the nearby parish grammar school.

All of this meant a great deal of extra work for the minister. Besides supervising the studies of his scholars, he had to make sure that they were provided with adequate heat and food at the parsonage, where most of them lived during the school term. Clearly he needed a woman to help him run the college—either an experienced housekeeper, or better still, a pretty and efficient young wife.

It was high time, anyway, that he thought of matrimony. He was already thirty-seven, and if he was ever to raise a family, he didn't have a great many years to delay.

During the summer of 1752, the Reverend Aaron Burr saddled his horse and rode north from Newark to Stockbridge, Massachusetts. His destination was the home of an elderly friend and colleague, the Reverend Jonathan Edwards.

In the thirteen American colonies there was no more brilliant theologian or philosopher than Jonathan Edwards. A famous Puritan preacher, he had published numerous books of sermons, as well as a variety of essays on different religious questions. He

was the first American writer to gain a European reputation. But it was not to discuss philosophical or religious matters that the Reverend Burr rode north to
New England; Jonathan Edwards was also the father
of eleven children, and several years before, his third
daughter, Esther, had made a great impression on the
Reverend Burr.

The visitor from New Jersey remained only three
days at Stockbridge. In that brief time he spoke per-
suasively to Esther, who agreed to marry him. A few
weeks later she arrived in Newark, accompanied by
her mother, and on June 29, 1752, the Reverend
Aaron Burr and Esther Edwards became man and wife.

Although Esther was only twenty-one, some sixteen
years younger than her husband, their marriage was a
happy one from the start. In 1754 their first child was
born; they christened her Sarah, but throughout her
life she was always called Sally by her friends and family.

Meanwhile, it was decided that the Newark parsonage provided too little space for the growing college. A new site was selected, about forty miles away,
in the village of Princeton. Plans were made to collect
funds for both a college dormitory there to hold a
hundred students, and also for a house where the college president and his family would live.

The Reverend Burr had more cares than ever to
occupy him now. By February, 1755, construction had
begun on the dormitory in Princeton, and a fund-rais-
ing campaign to pay for the work was in full swing.
Much of the time the minister was away from home.

Esther missed him, as she wrote in her diary and in her letters to her family in Stockbridge, but she had a cheerful disposition and usually managed not to feel too discontented during his frequent absences.

If there was any cause of friction between the married couple in the parsonage, it came about because of the husband's wish to improve his wife's inadequate formal education. He himself was a very learned man, well read in the classics and the Scriptures, while Esther, like almost every woman of her time, had little schooling. Her spelling was atrocious, her writing ungrammatical, and she did not know how to speak or read a foreign language. There was, the Reverend Burr realized, a French teacher in residence at the college whom he had hired to instruct the boys. Why shouldn't this teacher give Esther a few lessons as well?

But the idea did not appeal strongly to Esther. As she wrote in her diary, ". . . we have a French master in the house with us. He is learning the scholars French. . . . Mr. Burr has a mind . . . I should learn, but I have no time. . . . The married woman has something else to care about besides learning French . . . tho if I had time I should be very fond of learning."

At any rate, the lessons were soon discontinued. Esther Burr had been busy enough, caring for Sally and helping her husband manage the domestic affairs of the college. Before long she was even busier. On February 6, 1756, in the Newark parsonage, she gave birth to a second child, a son, named Aaron Burr in honor of his father.

It hardly seemed likely that the infant would sur-

vive his first year. He was gravely ill twice—shortly
after he was born, and again six or seven months later.
On the second occasion his mother had carried him off
to Stockbridge to visit her family. When they returned
to Newark, young Aaron contracted a throat infection
and ran a high fever. A doctor was called to the parsonage and declared that he would not survive the
night. But in the morning the despairing parents were
relieved to see that the doctor had been mistaken;
Aaron was still alive, and began to recover slowly. It
was many weeks, though, before the last symptoms of
his illness had disappeared.

Then, in December, 1756, the college buildings
were finished, and the Reverend Burr left Newark and
moved to Princeton. If anything, he had even more
work to do than before, supervising his students,
riding away to distant towns to solicit funds, and set-
tling himself and his family in their new home.

Esther was no less occupied, but she still found time
to write now and then in her diary. In one entry she
described her small son. It was a perceptive and revealing description.

"Aaron is a little, dirty, noisy boy," his mother
wrote of him when he was about a year old, "[and]
very different from Sally almost in everything. He be-
gins to talk a little; is very sly and mischievous. He has
more sprightliness than Sally, and most say he is handsome, but not so good tempered."

Then she concluded: "He is very resolute, and requires a good governor to bring him to terms."

A strong-willed little boy who needed the firm but

loving guidance of his gifted father—a guidance which, unfortunately, he was not to have.

During a few more weeks, the Reverend Aaron Burr, his wife and their two small children lived happily together. Then, one after another, an almost unbelievable number of tragedies struck the family.

In August, 1757, the Reverend Burr rode north to Stockbridge to discuss religious and educational matters with Jonathan Edwards, his eminent father-in-law. The trip in the summer heat proved taxing. Nevertheless, as soon as he had returned home to Princeton, he departed again.

This time he went to nearby Elizabethtown, to visit his friend Jonathan Belcher, the Governor of New Jersey. While staying at the governor's house, word reached the Reverend Burr that the wife of a close friend had died, and he hurried off to conduct the funeral service. Afterward he returned to Princeton, his energies even more depleted than when he had left.

At home he fell sick and ran a slight fever, but allowed himself no time to rest or recuperate. In a day or so he rode away again, this time to Philadelphia, to make further efforts to raise funds for the college. Returning home after a few days, he was shocked to learn that his friend the governor had died during his absence. Scarcely pausing to greet Esther and the children, he rode off once more to Elizabethtown to preach Governor Belcher's funeral sermon. By the time he returned to Princeton he was utterly exhausted.

He became violently sick, ran a high fever, and grew delirious. Gradually he fell into a coma. On September 24, 1757, he died in the president's house at Princeton, on the grounds of the little college he had done so much to establish.

Fever and disease, including outbreaks of smallpox, soon appeared everywhere in the colony. First it was little Aaron's turn to fall sick. For a time he ran "a slow fever," but eventually recovered. Then Esther's father, Jonathan Edwards, arrived in Princeton. He had been appointed the new president of the college, to succeed his late son-in-law, but his tenure was very brief. He was vaccinated for smallpox, fell ill, and died of the disease in Princeton, only two months after assuming his duties.

Aaron Burr's father and grandfather were now dead; his mother did not survive them long. Sixteen days after the death of the Reverend Jonathan Edwards, Esther Burr was dead of smallpox, too.

Shortly afterward, Aaron and Sally were taken to Philadelphia where, it was believed, the epidemic was less severe. They were placed in the temporary care of Dr. Shippen, an old family friend. Finally, in September, 1758, their grandmother, Sarah, Jonathan Edward's widow, came south from Stockbridge to take charge of the two orphaned children. Her plan was to return with them to the Edwards' home in Massachusetts, but she had hardly arrived when she too fell sick, lingered less than three weeks, and followed her husband to the grave.

Sally and Aaron Burr, now four and two, had lost their grandmother, grandfather, mother and father, all within the space of thirteen months.

At least in a material way the orphans were fortunate. From their father they inherited considerable property. With reasonably prudent management, there always would be enough money to provide for their needs. But there was no one left to provide them with the warmth and security of a happy home. For Aaron particularly, this was to prove a grave misfortune.

What sort of man he might have become if either his father or his mother had lived, one may only surmise. Deprived of their love and understanding, he became, in time, wily, self-centered and cynical, a man whose extraordinary gifts too often were used only for selfish ends. It was as though he had received so little affection as a child that after he grew up he had little affection to bestow on a hostile world.

2.

Student Days

AFTER THE DEATH of their grandmother in Philadelphia, the responsibility for raising Aaron Burr
and his sister fell to their oldest uncle, the Reverend
Timothy Edwards. The two children were taken to his
home in Elizabethtown, New Jersey, and soon were
established there as members of his family.

Children in eighteenth-century America, especially
in a strict Puritan household like that of the Reverend
Edwards, often lived under conditions that would
seem harsh and tyrannical today. They were prayed
over for their sins and beaten for their misbehavior.
They were taught to pay fulsome homage to their
elders, and were expected to rise each time their own
parents entered a room. If a boy encountered a minister or some other august person on the street, he was
obliged to remove his hat, bow deferentially, and remain utterly motionless until that august person had
made his way past.

For Sally Burr, life in Elizabethtown with her Uncle Timothy was endurable. She was a docile, good-natured child who created no problems for her guardian, and so she rarely suffered his displeasure. A young scholar was hired for her and Aaron, a Mr. Tappan Reeve, who taught them their first lessons. As Sally grew up she turned into a pretty young woman, and little by little she and Tappan Reeve fell in love. When she was seventeen they were married. Still later, Reeve became an able lawyer, and then a judge of the Supreme Court of Connecticut.

For young Aaron, though, life with the Reverend Timothy Edwards was a stormy affair. His uncle was a strict, humorless churchman, with little love of children. He believed that a boy like Aaron learned more from discipline than from kindness, and that the harsher his punishment, the more likely it would be that his soul would achieve a state of grace. Employing such notions, it was hardly surprising that the Reverend Timothy Edwards soon had a small but determined rebel on his hands.

The war between nephew and uncle was waged incessantly, year after year. At the age of four, Aaron disappeared from home. He was angry, and simply left the house and hid from his elders while they searched for him up and down the neighborhood. Somehow, as small as he was, he managed to elude them for three or four days.

At the age of eight, he incited his uncle to a pitch of fury. On a July afternoon he happened to climb a cherry tree in his uncle's garden. Peering out of the branches, he saw a prim, high-minded old Puritan lady, dressed in her best silk gown, heading up the garden walk on her way to seek spiritual comfort from the Reverend Timothy. The temptation to throw a few cherries at the stern-faced visitor was too great to resist. The cherries were flung at their target with considerable success, and a high-pitched voice registered a shriek of protest. Before long, young Aaron was summoned to his uncle's study. The Reverend Timothy then delivered a particularly long lecture on his sinful conduct and the enormity of his crime, and this was followed by a ten-minute prayer for his redemption. Finally he received his usual beating—or, as Burr himself described it in later years, "he licked me like a sack."

But prayers and beatings did little to quell Aaron's independent spirit, and when he was ten he decided to run off to sea. He stole away from home, and reaching New York, walked along the wharves of the bustling seaport until he found a ship that needed a cabin boy. He was hired, and for a short time worked and slept aboard the ship while the captain and crew made ready to sail.

One afternoon, as he was working on the quarter-deck, he saw an all-too familiar, black-clad figure striding along the wharf. Aaron didn't hesitate. He leapt for the rigging, and before Uncle Timothy could reach him, was thirty feet above the deck, safe among the spars and ropes.

His uncle ordered him to come down at once. Aaron politely refused. He knew that the minister was too old and ungainly—and far too dignified—to attempt to climb the rigging to catch him. So he remained aloft, while his uncle softened his voice and, instead of commanding, *requested* Aaron to *please* descend like a sensible child. But Aaron again refused. By slow degrees they began to parley, though as equals now rather than as uncle and nephew. At last, when the Reverend Timothy—whose promise could be trusted, because a minister never went back on his word—had pledged that no punishment would be dealt out *this* time, Aaron agreed to give up the sea and return home to his schoolwork.

One of the greatest consolations of Aaron Burr's childhood, and indeed of his entire life, was reading. He had a swift and inquiring mind, and from the very beginning devoured books of every description as they came to hand. By the time he was eleven, he was sure that he was ready to enter college, and applied for admission to the next freshman class at the College of New Jersey.

Entrance requirements were considerably less exacting then than they are today; a knowledge of Greek grammar and the ability to read Virgil in Latin were two of the most difficult standards to be met, and Aaron knew that he could easily meet them. But his appearance was against him; he was a short thin boy who looked, if anything, younger than his age. Despite his unusual precocity, he was still clearly a child, and children did not customarily attend college. His application was refused.

For two years he continued to study in Elizabethtown, and when he was thirteen, applied again to the college in Princeton. This time, perhaps in deference to the memory of his father, the Reverend Aaron Burr, he was admitted to the sophomore class by President Witherspoon.

As a college student, Aaron Burr did not particularly distinguish himself. He did his classwork easily enough and earned high grades without great effort, but he was not an outstanding scholar. For recreation he gambled occasionally for modest sums, and joined a literary-debating society; when a religious "revival" swept the college during his senior year he did not participate in it, despite the urging of some of his classmates and teachers, who reminded him of the important ministers and preachers among his forebears, including his own father and grandfather.

But Aaron Burr already was a cool, logical youth, and outbursts of religious fervor did not appeal to him or suit his temperament. If he was attracted to anything, it was not to religious turmoil but to thoughts of war and military glory. Like many young men in the American colonies, he had adopted Frederick the Great of Prussia as his personal hero, and had read all that he could find on the subject of the king's military campaigns.

Aside from his unusual precocity, the oddest thing about Aaron Burr at this early period was his method of correspondence. When he wrote to his friends he often used a code, as though fearful of revealing too much of his private thoughts or feelings. It was true that the mails of the time were likely to be tampered with, and that there were busybodies everywhere who had no compunction about reading letters addressed to somebody else. It was also true that in later years—

both during and after the Revolutionary War—such statesmen as George Washington, Alexander Hamilton and Thomas Jefferson occasionally used codes or ciphers in their private correspondence. Nevertheless, it was a curious habit for a young man to have developed so early in life, for the letters he was writing at Princeton and Elizabethtown contained nothing beyond the idle gossip of the moment. Yet, apparently, caution and mistrust were deeply ingrained in Aaron Burr. He was habitually secretive, and loved to deal in mystery and intrigue, even when the matter in question required no dissemblance.

Among Aaron Burr's contemporaries at Princeton were many young men of exceptional talent who, in later years, distinguished themselves in a number of fields. Burr's special friend, Matthias Ogden, became, during the Revolutionary War, a brigadier general; Samuel Spring eventually became a popular minister and Jonathan Dayton a Senator from New Jersey. The future President of the United States, James Madison, was a student at Princeton at the time; so was New York's future Chief Justice, Brockholst Livingston, and New Jersey's future Governor, William Patterson.

But all of their various careers still lay far ahead of them. For the present there was only the carefree academic life in the rural village of Princeton, and then, finally, the day of graduation itself.

This must have been one occasion when Burr felt extremely strong emotions. Almost alone among his friends and classmates, he had neither father nor

mother to attend the ceremonies, to listen as he delivered his Latin Oration, and to smile with covert pleasure at his youthful achievements. On that account,
the day must have been a sorrowful one.

But as the ceremonies proceeded, there must have
been considerable satisfaction, too. Accepting his
diploma, Burr knew that he was the youngest member
of his class by several years, and that he had accomplished without the slightest difficulty every academic
task he had set for himself.

Perhaps he had accomplished these tasks a little too
easily. And perhaps, mingled with his satisfaction,
were the first stirrings of pride and ambition—a pride
which already told him that he was more gifted than
any of his fellows, an ambition which one day would
urge him to demonstrate that fact before the entire
world.

3.

Religion or the Law?

ARON BURR graduated from the College of New Jersey at the age of sixteen, in September, 1772. As with any young man from a wealthy colonial family, two principal careers—the Church or the Law —were open to him. But because of his youth and inherited private income, there was no immediate need for him to choose between the two. For the time being, his guardian, the Reverend Timothy Edwards, agreed that he might just as well study what he pleased and improve his mind in his own fashion. This young Aaron Burr did, dividing his time agreeably between Elizabethtown and Princeton.

For a year he followed his own bent, and because his mind was immensely active and curious, he read a great variety of books which he added to his private library. Among other writers, he made the acquaintance of Diderot, Voltaire and Rousseau, whose works already had produced a vast intellectual ferment both in Europe and America.

Young Burr did not spend all his time in study, though. He was anything but a spiritless pedant who preferred the pages of a book to the company of men —or women. Indeed, he enjoyed both books and society equally, and never willingly did without either if he could help it. While at Princeton and Elizabethtown he was out in "society" a great deal. In his letters to his friends he acknowledged that, despite his youth, he already was considerably attracted to women. It was to be a lifelong interest—and one of his failings— though the details of many of his amorous adventures were never disclosed by the secretive Burr. But at the age of sixteen and seventeen he was flirting with the attractive young women around him and apparently enjoying at least the superficial favors of several.

He did not confine himself solely to polite teas and suppers for amusement. He was an active, restless youth who liked being out of doors; he hunted, fenced, and rode horseback much of the time. His favorite sport was sailing. When at Elizabethtown with Matthias Ogden, he often navigated the nearby waters of the Kill van Kull until every cove, harbor and sandbar along the shore was familiar to him. He was always at home on the water, and there were several times during his later life that his knowledge of boats and navigation came in handy.

For almost a year this idyllic existence continued, and then the day came when he had to consider his future career. He would have to become either a minister or a lawyer—which shoud it be?

There was no doubt what the Reverend Timothy Edwards, his guardian, thought of the matter. Family tradition indicated that Aaron should follow in the footsteps of his father and grandfather. It was an opinion concurred in by numerous uncles and other relations on both sides of the family.

Even Burr's friends agreed that he should study for the ministry. Samuel Spring, his college classmate, now a young theological student himself, wrote him a letter to that effect. "Remember," Spring said, "that [your becoming a minister] was the prayer of your dear father and mother, and is the prayer of your friends to this time."

The pressure from all sides was too strong to resist. No doubt with many inner misgivings, the youth agreed to a course of study that would lead to the ministry.

The man he chose to study with was the Reverend Joseph Bellamy, a former student of Jonathan Edwards, and now a distinguished Calvinist preacher. The Reverend Bellamy lived in Bethlehem, Connecticut, where he had turned his house into a school for theological students. In the autumn of 1773, Burr left New Jersey and went to Bethlehem to study the Presbyterian theology of his forefathers.

The Reverend Bellamy was a successful teacher, and often employed a device he called the "Socratic method" in his classes. That is, he and a selected pupil, having implicitly decided beforehand what the solution to a particular religious problem was, would attempt to demonstrate the inevitability of that solution through a series of questions proposed by the one and answers offered by the other. Usually Dr. Bellamy played the first role, that of "Socrates," and his pupil the second role, that of his "disciple."

The Socratic method had worked well enough with Bellamy's pupils because they already agreed with their teacher's conclusions. But Burr was one pupil who did not. To the contrary, he discovered within a short time that he disagreed with any number of the Reverend Bellamy's religious ideas. To make matters worse, Burr had a more logical mind than his teacher and was more fluent and persuasive in debate. Before many weeks had passed, Burr, in youthful glee, was able to write to his friend Ogden that he had Bellamy "completely under [his] thumb." No doubt the statement was all too true.

After several months of theological study, Burr decided what he must have suspected from the beginning: he was not a suitable candidate for the ministry. He could no longer accept the Calvinistic doctrine of his father and grandfather; he had come to believe that there were many religious paths, not merely one, and he could write that he thought "The road to heaven [is] open alike to all." Early in the summer of 1774 he bade a friendly good-bye to the Reverend Bellamy and left the latter's theological classes at Bethlehem.

Having turned away from the religion of the Burrs and the Edwardses, he knew that his only recourse was to begin the study of law. Several of his relatives were eminent in that profession too. So he asked his guardian, the Reverend Timothy Edwards, whether he should study with another uncle, Pierpont Edwards, or with his own brother-in-law, Sally's husband, Tappan Reeve.

The Reverend Timothy had long since despaired of his troublesome nephew and had grown weary of his independent and vexatious conduct. Aaron's abandonment of the religious life must have been the last straw to the Reverend Timothy. He wrote to his nephew in the coldest manner, declaring that "[your decision is] a matter of indifference to me. I would have you act your pleasure therein." Relieved of the need to satisfy his guardian, Burr selected Tappan Reeve as his mentor. Shortly afterward he moved into the Reeves' house in Litchfield, Connecticut, where he was united again with his favorite relative, his sister Sally.

Life in Litchfield was extremely pleasant for young Burr. It was summer in New England, and there were far too many tantalizing diversions for a lighthearted lad of eighteen to settle down earnestly with his lawbooks. Burr devoted most of his time, instead, to writing jesting letters to his scattered friends, to reading, hunting, and riding, and to flirting with the pretty young women of the neighborhood.

By now he was a decided favorite with women. Though short—five-foot-six—his dark eyes, fair skin and light hair, good manners and graceful wit more than made up for his small stature. He even confided in a letter to Matthias Ogden that one young woman

in Litchfield had spoken to him seriously of love, passion and matrimony—which conversation had made
him feel extremely foolish and a bit uncomfortable.

It was, indeed, a pleasant, idle life. But it raised a
puzzling question. The year was 1774. The American
colonies, long in political turmoil, were on the edge of
open rebellion. Yet what effect, if any, did the stirring
events of the times have for young Aaron Burr?

The answer can only be judged by inference. Characteristically, Burr did not commit his thoughts or
feelings on these matters to paper. His letters do not
contain a single reference to the major events of the
day.

The very fact that he was content to remain in Litchfield, far from the centers of conflict, and that he made
no effort to participate in Patriot affairs reveals a
lack of interest in the larger world. Here, then, was no
fiery radical like Samuel Adams of Massachusetts or
Patrick Henry of Virginia. Here was no Patriot like
Benjamin Franklin or John Adams, no political philosopher like young Thomas Jefferson or Alexander
Hamilton. The latter, almost the same age as Burr,
already was busy in New York as a Patriot pam-
phleteer.

As yet, Aaron Burr felt no desire for power or prestige. Perhaps he was too young, well-off, and content
to yearn for a role in public affairs. For the present
there was reading, the tentative beginnings of legal
studies, hunting, riding, and feminine companion-
ship.

In the letters of Burr there is only one incident
whose mention indicates the direction of his political

feelings. In August, 1774, a Patriot mob in neighboring Barrington attacked the house of a suspected Tory. Eight of the mob were arrested and brought to Litchfield under guard. The next day fifty horsemen assembled to ride into town and rescue the Patriot prisoners. Aaron Burr was one of the horsemen. That his sympathies that day were with the Patriot cause there can be no doubt.

But perhaps there was more involved than political fervor. Burr was drawn to action for its own sake. He was impetuous and daring, and he loved to throw himself into a fight. In August, 1774, he was disappointed in his craving for action. The fifty riders were stopped by the sheriff before they even could set out for the jail. To make matters worse, the would-be rescuers "all gave bond for their appearance," as Burr wrote, "to stand trial at the next court for committing a riot." And then they tamely dispersed.

Aaron Burr's growing desire for action was soon to be satisfied, however. In the following spring, word reached Litchfield of the pitched battle between the American colonists and British regulars near Boston. The Battle of Lexington had been fought; war was seen as inevitable. Burr, the indolent law student and admirer of Frederick the Great, wanted military fame. Exciting events were stirring in the east—and that was where he decided to go.

4.

The Drums of War

O N HEARING of the Battle of Lexington, Burr immediately sent a letter to Matthias Ogden telling him that the time had come to put aside their lawbooks and take up the profession of arms. Great military campaigns would soon begin and a marvelous opportunity for honor and glory lay directly ahead of them. Ogden was to leave Elizabethtown at once and hurry to Litchfield; then they would ride east together and volunteer to serve with the army which General Washington was gathering at Cambridge, on the outskirts of Boston.

The prospect of war and combat moved Burr intensely. Courage, he believed, was the highest human virtue, a soldier's calling the most exalted in the world. No one ever loved a bold enterprise more, especially if it required ingenuity, bravery, and physical endurance. Despite his polished manners, his passion for reading and reflection, his brilliantly cool and logical mind, he was a man of action. A born adventurer, he was stirred by risk and danger as by little else.

His friend Ogden, while sufficiently enthusiastic to volunteer for service, was not in a similar hurry to reach the theater of war. He wrote a calm letter in reply, saying there were personal matters he had to settle before he could join his friend.

This did not satisfy the impatient Burr. The Battle of Breed's Hill—to become known as Bunker Hill— had now been fought, American forces had stood up to regular British troops. Further delay was out of the question. The country was under siege, and they were needed. Burr left Litchfield and hastened south to Elizabethtown. He convinced Ogden there was not a moment to be lost. In a few days they were riding north to Cambridge, where they felt sure the American forces would welcome them cordially.

Their reception in camp, however, proved a disappointment. They presented their letters of recommendation to General Washington, but instead of being warmly received by the Commander in Chief, they were told their cases would be studied. In due time volunteer commissions might possibly be issued to them. No further encouragement was given, and they were dismissed.

Their reception was particularly galling to Burr's pride, but there was little reason for his resentment. General Washington simply had far weightier matters on his mind than the question of whether or not two young men from New Jersey should be accepted as volunteer officers.

The commanding general's problems were truly

immense. There were 17,000 soldiers in the American camp at Cambridge, most of them recent recruits who understood nothing of army life or discipline. Almost every military necessity was in short supply: muskets, ammunition, cannon, uniforms, shoes, tenting, stoves, bedding. The officers for the most part were as ill-trained as their companies. Some kind of order had to be provided, and in the midst of such chaos it was unlikely that two eager volunteers from New Jersey would seem of much importance to the general, no matter how great their youthful enthusiasm.

The days went by at Cambridge, but nothing happened. Apparently they had been forgotten. They sat in their tent with Samuel Spring, Jonathan Dayton and other college friends who had joined them in Cambridge. In their disappointment and idleness they condemned Washington for the wretched appearance of both camp and troops.

Nor could they understand why the general refused to renew the fighting with the British. A single bold attack, they declared, would surely drive the enemy clear out of the port of Boston. Why, then, wasn't the attack mounted at once? The answer was a closely held secret, known only to Washington and his senior officers. There wasn't enough ammunition in the American army to fight for an hour, much less to drive the Redcoats out of the city.

Soon Burr fell sick with a fever—probably from impatience and frustration as much as anything else. While he lay in his tent, an exciting rumor spread through camp. Colonel Benedict Arnold was at Newburyport, gathering an expeditionary force to invade

Canada and attack Quebec. Volunteer officers, as well as regularly enrolled troops, were to be used. The enterprise promised great benefits to the Patriot cause, as well as glory to the men who took part in it.

While Burr lay tossing feverishly in bed, Ogden and the others volunteered. They tried to keep him from learning what they had done, but after a day or two he had it out of them. Despite their protests he left his sickbed and volunteered. By the time he had received his commission as a volunteer officer who was to serve with Arnold's forces, his convalescence was over.

Before long, a number of letters to Captain Burr began to arrive in camp from various relations, urging, advising, imploring him not to take part in the Canadian expedition. Burr replied that he appreciated their solicitude, but he was going. Duty and patriotism called. Even the pleas of his sister Sally could not deter him.

While Ogden and most of the others traveled comfortably by carriage to Newburyport, some 50 miles to the north, Burr shouldered his knapsack and hiked there on foot. He was now a soldier and believed that soldiers on duty should not ride in carriages or live in luxury.

At Newburyport one final entreaty came from his family. A messenger bearing a letter from his Uncle Timothy Edwards arrived in camp. Burr read the letter and scowled. Uncle Timothy had written in his usual peremptory style. He *ordered* his nephew—who was still his ward—to give up the harebrained scheme. As Aaron's legal guardian he *commanded* him to return to Cambridge at once. He *must not go* to Canada with Arnold through hundreds of miles of unmapped wilderness. The march, to any sane person, was a hopeless folly, and if he would not return willingly to the vicinity of Boston, then for his own good he would be forcibly returned, in spite of himself.

Burr finished reading the letter, then said to the messenger, "Suppose I refuse to go, how do you expect to take me back? If you were to attempt it by force, I would have you hung up in ten minutes."

The messenger nodded silently. He gave Burr a second letter. This time, Burr's guardian used a softer tone. He expressed great fondness for his ward—a fondness which he usually had managed to conceal quite successfully during Burr's earlier years. Burr, however, was moved by his uncle's entreaties—or, in later times, he liked to claim that he had been moved. But he was not to be stopped by words of affection. He told the messenger to convey his intentions to his uncle—that he was going to march to Quebec with Arnold and his men, and nothing could stop him.

The messenger nodded silently again. Then, from a jacket pocket he took out a small bag of gold coins, handed it to Burr, and left the camp. The young captain, just nineteen years old, returned to quarters and eagerly began to prepare himself for what lay ahead.

5.

The Wilderness March

THE AMERICAN CAMPAIGN against Canada, which began during the autumn of 1775, was one of the most venturesome of the Revolutionary War. General Washington's strategy was as simple as it was bold. Two separate American forces were to be employed simultaneously, one in the west under General Richard Montgomery, the other in the east under Colonel Benedict Arnold.

The western force was to invade Canada by way of Lake Champlain and the recently captured Fort Ticonderoga. Its objective was Montreal where the British commander, Governor Guy Carleton, a skilled and experienced campaigner, had his headquarters.

While a part of Carleton's army was under siege at Montreal, Colonel Arnold and his men were to slip quickly and secretly through the north woods and descend on the unsuspecting British troops occupying the rugged fortress citadel at Quebec. It was Washington's hope that both Montreal and Quebec could be taken before reinforcements from England—said to be on the way in substantial numbers—could sail up the St. Lawrence River and relieve the beleaguered British garrisons. If this could be accomplished, the heartland of Canada would be in American hands. Canadian colonists, many of French descent, might well be persuaded to join in the war against Great Britain. In any event, the capture of Montreal and Quebec would mean that a grave threat to the northern flank of the thirteen American colonies had been permanently removed.

Such were the hopes of the Americans as the autumn campaign began. The stakes were large, and the play for them was vigorous. In the west, everything progressed smoothly. General Montgomery's troops had the easier and shorter invasion route. Advancing quickly through upper New York and meeting no unforeseen obstacles, they soon were approaching Montreal according to plan.

In the east, however, things went quite differently. To reach Quebec, Benedict Arnold and his men had to traverse a wild and little-known region of the northeast. Before it was over, their wilderness march had become one of the great sagas of hardship and endurance of the American Revolution.

Colonel Arnold's expeditionary force, consisting of almost 1,100 men, left Newburyport, Massachusetts, on September 18, 1775. The men sailed in eleven transports along the Atlantic Coast to the mouth of the

Kennebec River. Here they disembarked on September 20th and transferred their supplies and equipment into about 200 light, flat-bottomed boats for the ascent of the river.

Progress was slow but encouraging at first. The weather remained warm during the daylight hours, though at night there was frost on the ground and an ever-increasing chill in the air. Winter was approaching.

The soldiers were in good spirits. Burr had recovered his health and was elated. He was pleased with the soldiers assigned to him, most of them frontiersmen from Virginia and Pennsylvania who were thoroughly familiar with conditions in the wilderness. Burr knew it was fortunate they were, for each day, as the expedition traveled farther up the narrowing river, the country grew more wild and forbidding.

Burr was gratified to find himself as much at home in the woods as the rugged frontiersmen under his command. His knowledge of small boats was of practical use on the river. He was pleased with the company of his fellow officers, Ogden, Dayton, and Spring, who was serving as chaplain of the expedition—as well as with a new acquaintance, Major James Wilkinson.

Unfortunately, there is no record of the first meeting between Wilkinson and Burr, no diary or journal to describe what either young man may have thought of the other. That each recognized a kindred spirit in his new companion can hardly be questioned. During the years to come they were to remain on friendly terms, exchanging letters occasionally, until at last their dreams of wealth and power united them in a western adventure that could have sent both to the gallows.

His lifelong friendship with Wilkinson does not reflect much credit on the character of Aaron Burr. For in the familiar cliché "Birds of a feather flock together" there must be some measure of truth. And James Wilkinson was a very unsavory bird, indeed. Whenever his name appeared during the early history of the United States, it was always in connection with some underhanded scheme or highly discreditable action. He was an inveterate plotter, a chronic malcontent, a man utterly devoid of principles or personal honor. And Aaron Burr was to stay on excellent terms with him for more than a quarter of a century.

Burr cannot be excused, even in his youth, because of lack of experience of judgment, for he had already become an acute observer of his fellow men. During the wilderness march and the rest of the Canadian campaign, he formed a startlingly accurate opinion of his superior officer, Benedict Arnold, who was to betray his country a few years later.

"Arnold," Burr is known to have said, "is a perfect madman in the excitements of battle, and is ready for any deeds of valor; but he has not a particle of moral courage. He is utterly unprincipled, and has no love of country or self-respect to guide him. He is not to be trusted anywhere but under the eye of a superior."

It would be surprising if Burr, having understood the character of Benedict Arnold so completely, could have been greatly deceived by the character of James Wilkinson.

The truth is that Wilkinson appealed to the worst elements in Burr while men like Matthias Ogden and Samuel Spring appealed to the best. Burr was a highly complex individual, his personality a mixture of contradictory elements that often seemed to clash. By the time of the wilderness march he already was something of a schemer, an opportunist, a plotter. Yet at the same time he had a strong capacity for friendship, a real love of personal honor, and courage to a high degree. Few men in Benedict Arnold's band were braver or possessed more qualities of a good soldier. Now, along the banks of the Kennebec, these qualities were to prove extremely valuable.

After the first few days in the wilderness, it was obvious the expeditionary force had fallen into serious difficulties. Chiefly to blame were the maps which had been issued to Arnold and his officers. Time and again these maps failed to disclose the true nature of the terrain or the formidable obstacles which lay across the line of march. As a result, Arnold and his men found themselves falling further and further behind schedule. The chance of reaching Quebec in time to surprise the garrison was growing slimmer. Worse still, the first days of the northern winter were drawing near.

As they struggled toward the headwaters of the Kennebec, the river grew more shallow, the current swifter. The boats, built hastily of green timber, began to leak. The men were soaked from dawn till dark. Even after they made camp each night the air remained so cold that their wet clothing failed to dry out completely in the feeble heat thrown off by the campfires.

Food supplies became water-soaked, too. Soon the flour was covered with a greenish mildew and the salt beef and mutton became increasingly rancid.

As the river grew still narrower, their rate of progress continued to slow; shoals appeared often, and there were numerous waterfalls. Again and again— more than thirty times in all—the boats had to be emptied of everything and carried, along with the supplies, around river obstacles.

Then it began to rain, and the hungry, tired men fell sick with colds and fever. Some contracted pneumonia and died.

By the time the headwaters of the Kennebec had been reached, the weather had been stormy for several days. The entire countryside was a swamp. Twelve miles ahead lay the next river. Weary, sick, half-starved, the men pushed on through tangled under-brush, around the base of an intervening mountain, then through bogs and morasses. Their feet soaked and painfully swollen, they carried the boats and equipment every yard of the way.

At last, after twelve miles of torture, the forward companies reached the dark, slow-moving waters of the Dead River, a small stream that ran northward toward the Canadian border. They set their boats in the water and paused briefly, before moving on. They grumbled about the rear companies, especially those under Colonel Enos which were supposed to bring up most of the expedition's food supplies.

They waited for the supplies as long as they dared, then resumed their journey. The Dead River proved to be so deep that poles couldn't touch bottom and were useless. So they were forced to disembark and inch along the banks, hauling the boats by hand.

Colonel Enos and his men never joined the forward contingents of the expedition. The colonel had decided there was no chance of reaching Quebec and effecting its capture. So he and his men turned back, taking with them the food supplies that Arnold and the rest needed desperately.

Conditions continued to grow worse. One day there was a torrential rainstorm. Without warning a flash flood followed. The torpid river rose with stunning swiftness and tore between its banks, sweeping away boat after boat. All the cannon and most of the remaining food supplies were irretrievably lost in deep water.

On October 25th it began to snow. Winter was upon them, and they were still many miles from their goal. At night they huddled around what fires they could build with damp wood and tried to keep from freezing. Their rations gave out completely. Faced with starvation, Burr and the others killed the dogs which had accompanied the expedition as pets. They chewed bits of leather, belts, extra boots, gnawed at anything that promised nourishment. Soldiers were left where they died, for none of the living had strength enough to bury the dead.

Bearded and footsore, wild-eyed and in rags, they reached the end of the Dead River. One final barrier stood across their path. They lifted the last few remaining boats and carried them overland, up the steep hills of the Boundary Mountains, then staggered down the opposite slope—into Canada. Coming to Seven Mile River, they struggled to pole their boats forward, and at last arrived at their rendezvous with the forward scouts at Chaudière Pond. They had reached their first goal, after seven weeks of incredible toil and hardship. They numbered 500 men, less than half the force that had left the mouth of the Kennebec so cheerfully more than forty days before.

Matthias Ogden had managed to keep a sketchy journal while on the march. He and the others continued to Sartigan on the Chaudière River, and there relief finally came. Colonel Arnold, in advance of the main body of troops, had stopped at a French-Canadian settlement and purchased food supplies. On November 2nd the supplies were delivered, and Ogden recorded the event in his journal.

The food, Ogden wrote, was "the finest sight my eyes ever beheld. . . . Scarce one of us but with tears of joy expressed the gratitude of his heart at seeing five horned cattle and two birch canoes loaded with mutton and flour brought forward by French men."

Burr, Ogden and the others ate and rested. Then the expedition, though sadly depleted, moved forward again. Quebec lay ahead beyond flat and settled country. If the prize could be seized, all of Canada might become a fourteenth rebel colony, an ally in the war against the King.

6.

Early Days at Quebec

DURING THE FIRST WEEK of November Arnold and his men marched toward the St. Lawrence River. By the 7th of the month the leading contingents had reached Pointe Levis, opposite the city of Quebec. It was six days later before the last of the men straggled wearily into the riverside camp.

By that time there was no chance of surprising the Quebec garrison. Arnold's slow progress through the northern woods had given ample time for rumors of his approach to reach the British. Worse still, Arnold had sent two messages from Chaudière Pond to General Montgomery in the west, and by ill luck both messages had fallen into enemy hands.

As soon as Governor Carleton learned that an American force was at Chaudière Pond and that Quebec, the key to Canada, was threatened, he left the defense of Montreal to subordinates and sailed with all possible speed to Quebec to organize its defense.

Meanwhile, the Quebec garrison was alerted. If the Americans were to take the city at all, it would have to be by direct assault.

Nevertheless, some cheerful news did reach Arnold and his men as they prepared to lay siege to the fortress city on the opposite shore. General Montgomery, they learned, had been extremely successful in the west during the first days of the campaign. He had entered Canada, captured the villages of Chambly and St. John's, and now was sweeping down on Montreal itself with every hope of taking it in one swift attack.

In the belief that aid would soon arrive from Montgomery, Arnold's troops prepared to cross the river and attack Quebec. Many difficulties beset them. The British had burned most of the available boats and taken the rest for their own use. In addition, the river was patrolled by two British warships, which sailed up and down below the fortress ready to warn the garrison of an attack.

Arnold and his men had learned, however, that the local inhabitants owned a number of small boats which the British had not discovered. They managed to buy enough of these to meet their needs. On the night of November 13th they pushed their boats into the river. They eluded the patrolling warships in the dark, reached the opposite bank safely, and landed at Wolfe's Cove. Before the British were aware of their presence, they had climbed to the Plains of Abraham outside the city walls and made their camp.

Now, having endured the hardships and misery of the wilderness march, the Americans came face to face with a new difficulty. They had reached their goal, the fortress of Quebec, yet as they began to inspect the walls of the fortress, they realized that they no longer possessed the strength to capture it.

With even a few of the cannon they had lost in swamps and flood, they might have blown a breach or two in the walls and stormed through them to take the city. With the original 1,100 men who had started up the Kennebec they might have attempted a direct assault, even without cannon. But they were reduced to only 500 able-bodied soldiers, who could not hope to carry the city without cannon to support them.

Arnold perceived their position was hopeless. Until artillery and reinforcements arrived from Montgomery, there was little point in remaining camped below the walls of the city. The order to retreat was given. On November 19th the expeditionary force withdrew from Quebec and retired to Pointe aux Trembles, about twenty miles to the west along the broad St. Lawrence.

The British controlled the river, so that it was impossible for the Americans to prevent Governor Carleton from reaching Quebec. With Carleton in the city, its capture promised to be even more difficult for the besiegers.

On November 20th Montgomery informed Arnold that Montreal had been captured, along with eleven British warships and a number of prisoners. Arnold again asked Montgomery for supplies and men. Then he sat back to await reinforcements.

As November drew to a close the weather became still colder. It snowed, and the entire countryside turned white. The men built shelters to protect themselves from the wind and found what warmth they could around their campfires. In their weakened condition and exposed positions, many fell sick. Smallpox broke out, and colds and influenza were commonplace.

By November 30th, when still no word had come from Montgomery, Arnold decided to send fresh dispatches to Montreal. "I have not had the pleasure of hearing from you for ten days," Arnold told the general. Then he repeated his request for food supplies, artillery and men.

Burr was chosen to travel to Montreal with the message. "Dear Sir," Arnold wrote, "this will be handed to you by [Captain] Burr, a volunteer in the army, and son to the former President of New Jersey College. He is a young gentleman of much life and activity and has acted with great spirit and resolution on our fatiguing march. His conduct, I make no doubt, will be sufficient recommendation to your favor."

Burr set off at once, but he did not reach Montreal. A few miles along the river he met General Montgomery, and accompanied him back to the camp at Pointe aux Trembles. The general had brought food supplies and cannon as Arnold had requested—but only 300 men. The rest of his troops had been left behind under Colonel Wooster to garrison Montreal and guard the British prisoners.

General Montgomery was heavyset, broad-shouldered, well over six feet tall. He and the diminutive Burr took an instinctive liking to one another. By that time Burr had lost much of his respect for Arnold. He felt that Arnold took too much interest in his own comforts while neglecting those of his soldiers. When

General Montgomery requested Burr's transfer to his staff, Arnold did not object.

The combined forces of Arnold and Montgomery, some 800 to 900 men, now marched back from Pointe aux Trembles to the outskirts of Quebec. When camp had been made, Burr moved into Montgomery's headquarters and became one of his two aides. He was by then a responsible leader of men—many of them twice his age—and a trusted officer serving directly under the commander in chief of the combined assault forces. Unquestionably military life suited him well.

7.

The Attack on the Fortress

AFTER JOINING General Montgomery's staff, Burr began to take part in the discussions of battle strategy for the capture of the city. Soon he suggested a plan which involved the scaling of one of the fortress walls at a redoubt called Cape Diamond.

General Montgomery thought so well of his young aide's plan that he gave him fifty men for training in the use of scaling ladders and other specialized equipment. But to Burr's intense disgust, the project was eventually abandoned. Afterward he insisted that if his plan had been followed, the attack on the city would have been successful.

In any case, the Americans could not delay their attack much longer. Although their chances of success looked faint, there was no way that they could substantially improve them. They had all the men and cannon they could collect. Inside the fortress the British would not grow weaker.

Indeed, if anything, the Americans were at the peak of their strength. The weather was becoming colder. Soon the dead of winter would be upon them. Disease continued to take its toll: smallpox, colds, fevers. And inside the town, warm and comfortable, the British could sit out the winter far more easily than their besiegers. Eventually, during the spring, reinforcements would arrive from Great Britain. Then the defending garrison, already twice as large as the force under Montgomery and Arnold, could not possibly be dislodged from the city.

One other consideration made an immediate attack necessary. Many of the American soldiers had volunteered for only a short period of service and their terms of enlistment would be over by the end of the year. No one could doubt their patriotism. When January 1st came, they were going to leave the ranks and start home—and nothing was going to stop them.

This problem of American volunteers and their terms of enlistment arose again and again throughout the war. Each time it caused Washington and his scattered field commanders endless problems. Sometimes it even compelled them to commit their armies to battle before they were ready.

The plan that finally was selected by General Montgomery for the attack on Quebec was a desperate one, but under the circumstances it was probably as sound as any that could have been adopted. A surprise two-pronged assault was to be made, one led by Arnold, the other by Montgomery. Several small forces were to be used as decoys at scattered points around the city where the men would shout and fire a few muskets to distract the enemies' attention from the real attack. It was further decided that the assault had to be made at night and under cover of a snowstorm.

The weather remained clear and cold, however, until almost the last possible moment. Then, on New Year's Eve, just hours before many of the soliders were to end their terms of enlistment, a howling snowstorm struck out of the northeast. General Montgomery promptly gave orders to form the attack.

Some 500 men followed Benedict Arnold through the snow and attacked at a defense position known as the Sault au Matelot barrier. The defenders there had been kept on the alert. They greeted the Americans with heavy small-arms and cannon fire. Arnold was hit by a musket ball and fell, his leg shattered and bleeding. Captain Daniel Morgan, at the head of a small company of Virginia riflemen, took command of the assault, charged the barrier, and breached it.

The defenders fled. Morgan, leading a handful of men, raced on to a second barrier. Here the defenders were mostly militiamen and sailors rather than British regulars. They had been celebrating New Year's Eve and were inside their barracks, many of them drunk.

One guard at the barrier was sober, though. He saw Morgan's men approaching through the swirling snow. As he turned to flee, he fired one of the loaded cannon. The British guards stumbled out of the barracks, fired a round or two, then fled into the town. But the cannon shot had discouraged most of the American soldiers. As Morgan began to pursue the British again, he found he was almost alone.

Within a few minutes, Daniel Morgan went to the very edge of the Upper Town—the heart of the citadel —and met no opposition. The city, he could see, was in complete confusion. There was no discipline or organized defense. Quebec was open to the attackers —but they had to strike now, while they had the chance.

Hurrying back to lower ground, Morgan urged an immediate assault on the Upper Town. Instead, there were further delays. Other officers urged caution. They said it would be better to wait for reinforcements. Only much later was Morgan finally able to advance toward the Upper Town again. By then it was too late.

The British were ready. Panic had given way to calm. Morgan's force met heavy fire and was cut to pieces, and Morgan himself taken prisoner. Had he been able to act at once he could have pushed his way into the citadel. Then, by sheer daring, he might have captured the heart of the fortress before the British officers had reorganized their terrified men. But caution had prevailed, precious minutes had been allowed to pass, and a priceless opportunity for the Americans was gone forever.

Meanwhile, the second arm of the assault had moved into action. About 300 men under General Montgomery made their way along a narrow path by the river, moving as stealthily as possible in the hope of catching the defenders off guard. Montgomery led the way. Burr, John McPherson, the general's other aide, and their Canadian guide followed close on the general's heels.

The narrow path they were compelled to use was so filled with snowdrifts and rough mounds of ice that their progress was very slow. At last they reached the first wooden barricade. There was no sound from the defenders above in the blockhouse guarding the entrance to the citadel.

Carefully they crawled up to the wooden pickets where carpenters sawed through four of the sharpened stakes. The howling wind drowned the noise of the saws. The general, Burr, McPherson and the rest wriggled through the hole between the stakes. Then they began to inch their way up the cliff path to the second line of wooden pickets.

Again the carpenters came forward and sawed a passage through the stakes. Again Montgomery, Burr and the rest of the column edged silently through the gap. Then they crept up the path, higher and higher on the cliff. They came to a turning in the path. Around the next corner, just out of sight, the guide whispered, stood the British blockhouse. It guarded the approach to the Upper Town.

A third time they edged forward. They turned the corner, the general first as always. For a few more seconds all was still. Burr, McPherson, the guide, followed one by one. Then a voice rang out in the dark.

The British had been waiting for them. A shot was fired. Then a second.

Montgomery threw himself forward up the path, directly at the firing guns. "Push on, my brave boys!" he shouted. "Quebec is ours!"

They were his last words. A hail of small-arms fire and cannon shot flew down on the Americans. Montgomery's huge body pitched forward. He was killed instantly, shot through the head. McPherson, the Canadian guide and a dozen other men at the head of the column were cut down in a few seconds of slaughter. Only one soldier survived the fierce barrage.

Burr found himself on the path, untouched. He turned to rally the men. He shouted that he would lead if they would follow. The soldiers huddled around the bend in the path, out of the line of fire. They knew that their general had been killed and were afraid to make a new assault on the block-house.

While Burr stood in the open, within sight of the blockhouse cannon and pleaded with the men, Colonel Campbell, second in command, came up from the rear. He decided that the blockhouse was impregnable—a decision with which the rest of the officers were all too anxious to agree—and ordered a retreat down the cliff path to safety. The men turned and ran pell-mell, leaving Burr alone on the path with the bodies of Montgomery and the others.

Colonel Campbell's decision, made either through fear or simple misjudgment, was an unfortunate one. Even while he was making it, the British troops around the corner of the path were pouring out of the blockhouse. They fled by a rear door, sprinted full speed up the hill, and left the way open to the attackers to enter the Upper Town.

But only Burr remained on the field. He hesitated, knowing it would be madness to follow the fleeing British alone. Then he hoisted General Montgomery's huge body across his thin shoulders and began to stagger down the cliff path after his retreating men.

Soon the British realized that they were not being pursued and returned to the blockhouse. All they could see below was a single American floundering along the path to the river through the drifts of snow, a dead man slung across his shoulders. The British soldiers left the blockhouse and, shouting, began to race after Burr.

Fearing he would be captured, Burr had to drop the general's body in the snow and run to safety. For a minute or two—like Daniel Morgan at another part of the fortress—he had been ready to burst into the Upper Town and perhaps to capture the heart of the city. The decision of Colonel Campbell, though, had drawn the troops away, there had been no one to follow him, and the second and final chance to capture the citadel had disappeared.

The Americans continued to besiege Quebec for a few months, but there was little fighting after the beginning of the new year. The main assault had failed. The dream of adding the colony of Canada to the American Confederation began to fade.

Although the Canadian campaign had accomplished far less than it might have for the American cause, it was a providential success for Aaron Burr. He had won the respect and praise of his superior officers. His bravery under fire during the attack on Quebec—especially his attempt to rally the troops after General Montgomery had fallen, and his efforts to carry the general's body away—brought his name to the attention of Patriots throughout the colonies and earned him a hero's renown. As a result, Benedict Arnold promoted him to the rank of brigade major.

His brother-in-law, Tappan Reeve, wrote to him from Litchfield.

Dear Burr, Amid the lamentations of a country for the loss of a brave, enterprising general, your escape from such imminent danger . . . has afforded us the greatest satisfaction. The news of the unfortunate attack upon Quebec arrived among us on the 13th of this month. I concealed it from your sister until the 18th, when she found it out; but, in less than half an hour, I received letters from Albany, acquainting me that you were in safety, and had gained great honor by your intrepid conduct.

Brigade Major Aaron Burr must have enjoyed his first taste of military glory. He was, by that time, just twenty years old.

8.

The New York Campaign

AFTER THE DEATH OF General Montgomery, Benedict Arnold assumed command of the American army in Canada. Arnold thought highly of Burr and found him a useful officer to have on his staff. Burr's dislike of Arnold, however, became only stronger during the tedious months when their little force remained encamped before Quebec.

Some of Arnold's military stratagems were certainly curious, and to the realistic Burr, they must have seemed absurd. As everyone in the American camp realized, the invading army was now far too small to have any hope of taking the city by direct assault. But perhaps, Arnold thought, the enemy might be starved into submission before the winter was out and General Burgoyne had reached the city with reinforcements.

So the Americans established a siege, cutting off supplies for the garrison, and waited for the enemy to surrender. When the British failed to show any inclination to do so, Arnold thought of another plan. He would "intimidate" Governor Carleton with a show of strength. The American troops paraded up and down below the fortress taunting the enemy. But the British merely ignored the parading Americans.

Finally Arnold decided to send a message to Carleton demanding that he surrender before they compelled him to. Having written the message, Arnold ordered Brigade Major Burr to carry it up to Carleton under a flag of truce.

Burr refused to, unless he knew what the message said. Arnold protested at first, then handed him the message. Burr read the message and told Arnold it was an insult to the British, a bombastic collection of insolent nonsense that would accomplish nothing. He refused to carry it to Carleton, saying that to do so would reflect on his own personal honor as an officer and gentleman. He went on to point out that no superior officer ever had the right to issue an *improper* order to an inferior—and nothing could have been more improper than the order to carry such a message to Carleton.

From that moment there was a mutual antipathy between them. Arnold's dislike of Burr must have increased further after another officer did carry the message to Carleton and returned with an answer couched in the heaviest sarcasm and scorn.

In April Burr accompanied Arnold when he left Quebec and traveled to Montreal to have his wounded leg treated. Burr's dislike of Arnold became intensified in Montreal. Moreover, he was tired of garrison life. Soon there would be renewed fighting in the south, in New York, Massachusetts, Connecticut, or New Jersey—and it was there that any ambitious and high-spirited young officer wanted to be. His friend Ogden had left Canada several months before. Returning home, he had obtained a regular commission and a promotion as well. Now he was Lieutenant Colonel Matthias Ogden of the 1st Jersey Battalion. Meanwhile, Burr languished in Montreal, a mere brigade major, with a volunteer commission.

Burr finally managed to be released and hurried south. In less than a fortnight he was in New York City where Matthias Ogden had previously spoken to General Washington on his behalf.

The general had recently arrived in New York and was quartered in the handsome Mortier Mansion at Richmond Hill. It was the house where Burr himself was destined to live during years of prosperity and success. On that early June afternoon in 1776, when he first saw it, Burr was attracted to the mansion—but not to its tenant, the Commander in Chief of the American army.

Washington agreed to have Burr attached to his staff, but Burr served for only a few days. Whether or not they disliked one another from the start is open to question. Washington probably did not form his unfavorable opinion of Burr until at least a year later, though he may have sensed in Burr an excessively ambitious pride.

Burr, for his part, did not greatly admire Washington, who had little knowledge of books and no interest whatever in discussing abstract philosophical or literary subjects. This surprised and disenchanted Burr, who had been accustomed all of his life to the society of intellectuals. The young brigade major found the general stiff, formal, and rather haughty. In his judgment, Washington was far too susceptible to the praise of flatterers and disliked the company of anyone who had an original and independent turn of mind.

Mainly, though, Burr thirsted for military action. As one of Washington's numerous aides, he had nothing to do but routine paperwork and no prospect of escaping to a regiment of the line. Even before joining the general's staff, Burr had written to an old family friend, John Hancock, who then was serving as President of the Continental Congress in Philadelphia. Burr stated that he wished to be assigned to active duty in the field; otherwise, he would retire from the army. He had not been Washington's aide for more than a week when Hancock arranged his transfer. He was assigned to the staff of General Israel Putnam, with the rank of full major, and the promise that before long he would see all the action he wanted.

The promise was soon fulfilled. Early in July, 1776, British ships entered New York harbor. They were followed by a huge fleet of transports and warships which came to anchor off Staten Island, to the south of Manhattan. By late July the British Commander in Chief, General Sir William Howe, had landed unopposed on Staten Island with an army of 35,000 well-disciplined troops. His plan was to take New York City, destroy Washington's army in the process, and crush the rebellion. All the odds, it appeared, were very much in his favor.

Washington's position on Manhattan was extremely unpromising. Not only was his army of 12,000 to 15,-000 men heavily outnumbered, but for the most part it was undisciplined, poorly equipped, and inexperienced. More than 3,000 were sick with dysentery or otherwise unfit for duty. Desertions were commonplace in the ranks, while among staff and field officers there was great bickering and jealousy.

Worst of all, Manhattan Island was nearly indefensible. The British fleet controlled the waters surrounding it. At any chosen moment their warships could sail up the Hudson and East rivers, all the way to Spuyten Duyvil, and prevent Washington's army from retreating north to the Bronx and Westchester.

Washington never lacked critics eager to advise him on military plans and strategy. Many of his officers, especially the younger ones, were dismayed at the general's announced intention to defend New York. Burr was one of the first to see the danger in the plan. Another was Captain Alexander Hamilton, serving in a field artillery company on Manhattan. Both Burr and Hamilton—whose lives would one day be inextricably linked—wrote letters to their superiors urging that the army be withdrawn to the safety of Westchester, leaving Manhattan undefended and open to the British.

Their advice went unheeded—naturally. For political reasons New York had to be defended. Washington realized that some of the colonies were lukewarm in their allegiance to the cause of Independence. The loss of New York City, particularly without a fight, might persuade those colonies to give up the struggle. There was no help for it—although the dangers were unmistakably grave, the defense of New York had to be carried out.

By mid-August the British plan seemed clear. Instead of attempting to take Manhattan by direct assault, General Howe would transfer his army to Long Island and march on Brooklyn Heights. From that high ground his guns could fire across the East River on the helpless American troops. Before long, the defenders would have to abandon New York.

In an effort to prevent the British from taking Brooklyn Heights, Washington decided to divide his small army and send part of it across the East River to Brooklyn and Long Island. On August 27th Howe struck. He transferred a major part of his forces to Long Island at a point considerably farther from the city than Washington had anticipated. Howe's troop landings again were unopposed, and soon, as American reinforcements were sent from Manhattan to Long Island, the two armies faced each other along a six-mile front.

Howe had one serious defect as a field commander: he was slow to move. Time and again during the war he had Washington's smaller forces in his grasp, only to let them slip free.

In the early phase of the Battle of Long Island, Howe observed that the Americans were too few to man their defensive line adequately. The American left flank, in fact, was hanging in the air.

During the night, Howe swung his own right flank around, and by early the next morning the American left had been hopelessly enveloped. General John Sullivan, in command of the American left, found that his men were being fired on from front, side and rear. General Stirling tried to come to Sullivan's aid, but he could not check the growing disaster. British veterans, using their bayonets, began to slaughter the green American troops, especially the New England militia companies which fled in panic. The entire line gave way. Generals Sullivan and Stirling were captured—to be exchanged several months later. More than 1,000 American soldiers were killed, wounded or taken prisoner, and the remnants retreated in disorder to previously prepared defensive positions on Brooklyn Heights. The rest of Long Island was left entirely in British hands.

Had General Howe followed up his victory with an immediate attack on the Americans crowded together in the trenches on Brooklyn Heights, he might have destroyed most of Washington's army.

But Howe delayed—as was his habit. Perhaps he remembered the attack the previous year on Breed's Hill outside of Boston. There, the British troops had suffered terrible casualties in driving against entrenched Americans. At Brooklyn Heights the Americans again were entrenched—and Howe chose to attack them only after regrouping his forces.

With half his soldiers pinned down on Brooklyn Heights, their backs to the East River, and the victorious British army facing them in overwhelming numbers, Washington's position was desperate. He was in a trap from which there seemed to be no escape. Howe's delay, however, gave Washington a faint chance. And then, when he needed it most, a stroke of good luck came to his aid.

A storm approached. The weather, already unseasonably cool for August, turned misty and even colder. In the afternoon Washington issued new orders. Instead of remaining on the Heights and strengthening their defenses, the American force of several thousand men, with all its equipment, would be ferried back to Manhattan under cover of rain and darkness.

The night proved to be pitch-black. The rain grew heavier. The wind rose providentially, drowning out the sounds of troops, horses, and oars. By dawn all of the soldiers, with most of their artillery and equipment, had safely crossed the East River to Manhattan. When General Howe inspected the lines the next morning he was astonished to see that the Americans had vanished. On the other side of the river Washington's army was once again united, and ready to do battle.

Burr had been on Long Island during the entire engagement. He had not been in the sector of the line where the fighting was heaviest. Back on Manhattan, however, he found a chance to distinguish himself, as he had in Canada.

The opportunity occurred on September 15th when General Howe, after a two weeks' delay, finally launched an attack on Manhattan. By then Washington had moved his headquarters to the northern portion of the island. With him were many of his troops and supplies, but a few thousand soldiers were still on the southern end of the island. Howe's landing at Kips Bay—near the present site of the United Nations—threatened to cut off the retreat of these men.

The landing of the Redcoats and the Hessians threw many American companies, especially the militia, into panic. There was confusion everywhere, but nowhere was it greater than at the extreme southern tip of Manhattan where a part of General Silliman's brigade was stranded. The troops had received no instructions. None of the officers had a clear idea of what was happening elsewhere or what they should do.

Colonel Henry Knox, Washington's chief of artillery, was the senior officer present. He naturally took command, and ordered the soldiers to man and defend a crudely built fort that happened to be standing in the neighborhood.

Burr rode up to the fort and asked who was in command. Knox came forward and said that *he* was. Burr then asked the colonel *why* he was there. Why hadn't Knox and his men begun to retreat northward to the lines in Harlem along with everyone else?

Knox said, frowning, that to retreat was out of the question. The British, according to rumor, already had driven west from Kips Bay to the Hudson River, thus cutting Manhattan in two and isolating everyone south of the line. Knox spoke testily; after all, who *was* this impertinent young major who dared to question a superior officer?

Knox then told Burr that his plan was to defend the fort to the bitter end and exact a high price in lives from the British.

Burr laughed openly. Defend the fort with *what?*

Where were Knox's provisions to withstand a siege? Where was his water supply, his dugouts and trenches to provide shelter from a cannonading? The British, Burr said, could take the place with one gun easily in a couple of hours. To remain was suicide. Burr told Knox he *had* to retreat, and quickly, north to Harlem.

Knox refused to budge. No pipsqueak of a major, looking as though he had just walked out of the nursery, was going to tell *him* what to do! No, indeed, sir, not for anything in the world was Colonel Henry Knox going to leave the fort!

What Burr did next was clearly an act of insubordination. Perhaps, under the circumstanes, it was excusable, though Burr always had a liking for independent action and was far too apt to defy higher authority whenever he felt the occasion justified it. In this case, he turned his back on the colonel and put the matter to the other officers and soldiers who had crowded around to listen to the debate.

"Stay here," Burr told them, "and by nightfall you'll all either be prisoners, rotting in a filthy prison, or you'll be hung up by your necks like dogs."

However, Burr went on, if they would obey his commands, he would get them out of the trap and save them from death or imprisonment. He knew the countryside well; he knew how to elude any British or Hessians who might have come between them and the American lines. He would lead them north to Harlem —and safety.

The men at the fort, including a sheepish Colonel Knox, followed Burr away with their arms and supplies. Burr led them over back roads, galloping ahead to scout for the enemy. He brought them unscathed through the British lines, with only a brief skirmish along the way.

It was a notable feat, but it never appeared in army dispatches. Probably Colonel Knox saw to that. The event, no matter how it was reported, would hardly throw a flattering light on his conduct. And so—officially—the deed was forgotten. But it was talked of widely in the ranks, and Burr's reputation throughout the army was considerably enhanced.

The incident had an interesting sidelight. Present at the fort with Burr was a fellow officer, as youthful as he, as ambitious and proud, and even more gifted. Alexander Hamilton had been at the fort when Burr arrived. To Hamilton's undoubted humiliation—for he thirsted after military fame as much as Burr—he had done nothing, while another young officer had seized the initiative, led the troops through the enemy lines, and covered himself with glory. In all probability it was an incident that Hamilton never forgot, and in later years it may have provided one more reason why he detested Burr.

The incident could give rise to another speculation. If Burr had not happened to arrive at the fort that day, how different would his own life and the history of the United States have been? Certainly most of the men inside the fort would have been killed or captured, and one of these men was Burr's future nemesis, Alexander Hamilton. Had Hamilton been killed, his political position would have been filled by somebody else twenty years later. When Burr's star rose, there would have been no Hamilton to bring it down—and who can guess how high it might have soared then?

But Burr did come to the fort that day, and did save young Captain Hamilton, as he saved the others. Years later, no more than a mile or two away, their paths would cross many times, their lives interwine, until their rivalry became so fierce and intractable that it brought death to one and hastened the ultimate ruin of the other.

9.

Malcolm's Regiment

AFTER THE RETREAT to Harlem, Burr continued to serve under Israel Putnam—"my good old general," as Burr referred to him privately. Putnam's troops saw action during the Battle of Harlem Heights, took part in the subsequent retreat from Manhattan to Westchester, and fought at White Plains, where once again the British won a victory.

Washington retired to New Jersey with the main part of his army, and then the American cause suffered a disaster. Fort Washington, guarding the Hudson River at the northern end of Manhattan, fell to the enemy with a great loss of soldiers, ammunition and guns. Fort Lee, across the Hudson in New Jersey, fell next. Washington's army, reduced to about 3,000 men, retreated south through New Jersey as the late autumn weather turned wet and cold. All the way to the Delaware River they were pursued by a British army of 8,000 troops under General Cornwallis.

Burr, still a major, went south with Putnam's troops as they helped fortify the American lines beyond the Delaware. On Christmas Night, 1776, Washington struck across the river and, catching the Hessians off guard at Trenton, won the first decisive American victory of the war. Within a few days the Americans scored another victory at Princeton. It was from this familiar village that Burr sent a bitter letter to his friend, Matthias Ogden, who had touched a sore spot by inquiring about Burr's prospects of becoming a colonel.

As to "expectations of promotion," I have not the least. . . . You need not express surprise at it, as I have never made any application, and, as you know me, you know I never shall. I should have been fond of a berth in a regiment, as we proposed when last I saw you. But, as I am at present happy in the esteem and entire confidence of my good old general, I shall be piqued at no neglect. . . . 'Tis true, indeed, my former equals, and even inferiors in rank, have [risen above] me. Assurance from those in power I have had unasked, and in abundance; but of these I shall never remind them. We are not to judge of our own merit, and I am content to contribute my mite in any station.

But, of course, Burr was not content at all. He knew —quite rightly—that he was entitled to a higher rank than the one he held, for again and again he had proved himself a fine leader of men. He also believed—quite wrongly—that Washington's personal bias was the real reason why he had not been promoted or given a combat assignment. Actually, the Commander in Chief had only a limited number of commissions at his disposal, and there always were far more candidates for promotion and combat assignment than there were vacancies.

In the meantime, General Putnam put Burr to work as an intelligence officer. Burr interviewed prisoners at New Brunswick and gathered information about Tory and British activities in New Jersey from a variety of agents whom he was empowered to employ. He displayed a remarkable talent for collecting such information, for he was a keen judge of certain types of men and knew instinctively whom to hire and which reports to depend on. Years later, as a politician, Burr was to display the same uncanny ability to ferret out enemy plans and information, so that at times he seemed to know more about what his rivals were doing than they knew themselves.

At last, after serving for almost a year as Putnam's aide, Burr received his long-overdue promotion. He was transferred to a regiment of the line, with the rank of lieutenant colonel. But for the excessively proud and ambitious young man—Burr still was only twenty-one, and one of the youngest colonels in the Continental Army—the promotion came far too tardily. His anger was not appeased. If anything, it only flamed higher.

The letter Burr wrote to General Washington, accepting his commission, proved an extraordinary example of presumption and pride.

I am constrained to observe that the late date of my appointment subjects me to the command of many who were younger in the service, and junior officers in the last campaign. . . . I would beg to know whether it was any misconduct in me, or any extraordinary merit in them, which entitled the gentlemen lately put over me to that preference? Or, if a uniform diligence and attention to duty has marked my conduct since the formation of the army, whether I may not expect to be restored to that rank of which I have been deprived, rather, I flatter myself, by accident that design?

It is probable that Washington's dislike of Aaron Burr dated from his receipt of this letter. To Burr's less ingratiating qualities—excessive self-assurance, ambition and pride—now could be added a kind of reckless insolence. Probably even more harmful to Burr's military career was his inability to conceal it.

Discontented or not, though, young Colonel Burr rode north to Ramapo, New Jersey, to join his unit, a newly recruited regiment of 260 men under the command of Colonel William Malcolm. Burr had not been in camp very long before he realized that both the colonel and his soldiers were totally unprepared for active service.

Malcolm's Regiment, as it was called, had been organized under the wasteful and corrupt system which continued to plague Washington and his generals throughout the Revolution. Because there was neither a national nor a local draft, the American army had to depend entirely on volunteers to fill its ranks. The only way to induce many men to enlist was to offer them a bonus. In addition, they had to be provided with uniforms, arms and other equipment. Since Congress did not possess adequate funds to meet these expenses, private citizens were encouraged to do what a weak government could not do for itself. A wealthy citizen was allowed to enroll volunteers, to pay their bonuses, and to provide their uniforms, tenting and muskets. In return for the money he'd spent, the wealthy citizen was flattered by having the company, battalion or regiment serve in his name. In addition, he received a commission appropriate to the size of the unit he had organized and was allowed to lead the unit as its commanding officer.

Malcolm's Regiment was a typical product of the system. The enlisted ranks were filled with "bonus grabbers," men interested only in obtaining as much money as they could for putting on their country's uniform. They had little thought of fighting or becoming good soldiers. The junior officers of the regiment were mainly young idlers from rich families who wished to dazzle the ladies by a display of military rank and the talk of war.

As for the commanding officer, Colonel Malcolm was a portly, good-natured, middle-aged family man, a merchant from New York City with strong Patriot feelings. But he had almost no taste for the life of a soldier. After a few days he perceived that young Colonel Burr was the answer to his secret and troubled prayers. Here was a real soldier with a fine record of service, a man capable of taking in hand his undisciplined soldiers and his incompetent young officers. Colonel Malcolm decided to shift the burdensome responsibility from his own shoulders to those of his second-in-command.

"You shall have all the honor of disciplining and fighting the regiment," he told Burr, "while I will be its father." And Colonel Malcolm promptly retired with his family to a house twenty miles away while Burr was left with the task of commanding the colonel's men.

Aaron Burr was in his element now. Whatever his detractors might say about his later activities, they never could deny that he was a brilliant soldier. He soon had Colonel Malcolm's undisciplined troops in hand, weeding out the incompetent junior officers and replacing them with able young men. He drilled and trained the enlisted ranks until, through firmness, patience and justice, he had taught them to take pride in themselves and their regiment.

A part of the regiment soon had a chance to prove itself in action. A large British force had gathered in Hackensack and now set out to plunder the countryside. Burr immediately rode off at the head of a contingent of his men to scout the enemy's approach. While Burr was advancing, he received an order from General Putnam to retreat to the nearby mountains with his entire regiment and avoid battle with the vastly larger enemy.

Burr, characteristically, thought his "good old general's" order ill-conceived. He told the messenger to return to Putnam and to say that he intended to find the enemy and see what the situation really was.

Burr concluded that "he could not run away from an enemy he had not seen, and that he would be answerable . . . for the [safety] of his men."

His insubordination once again was repaid with success. After a march of sixteen miles he reached Paramus, where he found the local militia in panic. Burr took command, restored the militia's confidence, and, using a few militiamen as guides, advanced on the enemy. He then bivouacked his men in a woods—they had marched thirty miles that day—and, while they slept, he himself slipped off to reconnoiter the enemy's position under cover of night.

He found the advance party of the enemy, sized up its strength and disposition, returned to his own bivouac, and aroused the sleeping troops.

Marching swiftly through the dark, they fell upon the sleeping British without warning, killed most of the advance party, and took the rest prisoner. Not a single American was lost in the attack.

By that time Burr had been without rest for more than twenty-four hours, but he immediately sent back to the regiment and ordered it to advance and meet him. His plan was to attack the main British force, but General Putnam prevented him from doing it. The general sent a second order telling Burr to rejoin the division at once. The tone of the order was extremely firm, and this time Burr was compelled to obey. Meanwhile the British, frightened by the stealthy night attack, retired hastily in the opposite direction, leaving behind most of the cattle and household goods they had stolen from the local citizens.

While serving in New Jersey with Malcolm's Regiment Burr began to overtax his physical strength. Long marches, insufficient rest, and an extremely spare diet combined to undermine his health.

During his days with the regiment, Burr also began to acquire the extravagant habits which were to have such a destructive influence on his later life. His army pay was small, and his personal income, though fairly substantial, was not unlimited. Yet he spent his money so freely that before long he was spending far more than he could afford.

At first, like so many vices, this profligacy had an appealing quality about it. He paid his friends' debts, he entertained his fellow officers, he bought better guns and even shoes and food for his men. Sometimes, when loaning money, he really was only giving it away.

Gradually he began to draw not only on his income but on his principal as well. He continued to spend freely, and in order to meet his obligations, tried his hand at an occasional speculation. Once he bought shares in a privateer, counting on the prizes it would capture to restore his dwindling fortune. But when, instead, the ship was sunk by the British, he lost his entire investment. Spending more, he grew poorer as the months went by—as did many other generous, free-handed and improvident officers in the Continental Army.

While undermining his health and spending most of his inheritance, Burr also involved himself in an unconventional and frustrating courtship. The woman concerned was Theodosia Prevost, who lived in Paramus, New Jersey. Undoubtedly Burr met her for the first time while on duty with his regiment in the vicinity of her home.

Theodosia Prevost came from a highly respected family. She was on friendly terms with the Shippens of Philadelphia, with George and Martha Washington, and numerous other prominent Americans. It was not her social credentials that disqualified her as a prospective bride for the brilliant young officer, nor was it her age—although she was ten years older than Burr. The difficulty was that she already had a husband. Lieutenant Colonel Jacques Marc Prevost was a British officer serving with His Majesty's forces in the West Indies. To make matters worse, she was the mother of the colonel's five children.

Yet Aaron Burr, at the age of twenty-one, fell under the spell of this charming older woman. He continued to love her more passionately and deeply with each passing month.

Had Burr been as dissolute and unprincipled as his friend James Wilkinson, he would never have allowed himself to court Mrs. Prevost. Other women far younger, prettier and richer than she had cast their nets to catch the eligible Colonel Burr. But though he needed money, he never considered a match for the sake of gain.

Mrs. Prevost, for her part, was greatly attracted to the self-assured, brilliant and energetic young man. They had many interests in common: a love of painting, reading, and the congenial exchange of intellectual ideas. That she began to return Burr's interest is certain. Yet she must have known even better than he that the chance of their ever marrying was extremely remote.

When orders came for Malcolm's Regiment to retire to the south and join Washington's army near Philadelphia, Aaron Burr left Paramus with a heavy heart. He had found the woman he wanted to marry, but what good could possibly come of it? To his cold and logical intelligence it was apparent that only by a miraculous stroke of good fortune could she become his wife and the mother of his children.

10.

The Conway Cabal

DURING THE last weeks of 1777, dissatisfaction with the progress of the war became widespread. There was considerable agitation to have General Washington's authority severely limited, or else to have him replaced as Commander in Chief by a more successful military leader. The choice of those who wished to see Washington removed was General Horatio Gates, "the Hero of Saratoga."

In October, 1777, at Saratoga, New York, Gates had won America's greatest victory of the war. The surrender of General Burgoyne's entire army had been engineered as much by Benedict Arnold as by anyone else, but credit for the victory had gone entirely to Arnold's superior. Almost overnight, particularly in New England, Horatio Gates became such a popular figure that not a word could be spoken against him.

At the same time that Gates was being idolized in

the north, Washington was suffering fresh reverses in the south. The autumn campaign of 1777 had seen a costly American defeat at Brandywine Creek and the subsequent military evacuation of Philadelphia. Congress was forced to flee the capital and move into temporary quarters at Lancaster, Pennsylvania. A few days later, General Howe and his army made a triumphal entrance into the largest city on the American Continent. In an effort to improve the situation, Washington launched an attack against Howe's lines at Germantown, but the attack was a failure. The loss of the American forts on the Delaware River not long afterward concluded the dismal autumn campaign in the south.

As a result of these defeats and failures, Washington's reputation as a military leader suffered a decline. The general, his enemies whispered, did nothing but lose battles, while General Gates did nothing but win them. Wouldn't it be common sense, then, to replace Washington with a better commander?

It wasn't long before a shadowy plot began to be formed to accomplish this. Rumors were circulated and letters exchanged, but matters had to be conducted with the greatest secrecy. Washington was still trusted by the majority of Patriot citizens, even by those who felt seriously disheartened with the results of the recent campaign. In addition, the most clearheaded and able of America's political leaders still held the unshaken conviction that Washington alone possessed the patience, selflessness and resolution to lead their struggling nation to its freedom.

The plot against Washington, called "the Conway Cabal," finally came to involve some disaffected members of Congress, some highly placed and ambitious military figures, particularly General Thomas Conway, General Thomas Mifflin, and General Gates himself, and numerous army officers of lower rank. Whether or not Aaron Burr was an active member of the cabal is not known for certain, though clearly his sympathy must have been with the plotters. It is known, however, that Burr's friend from the days of the wilderness march, James Wilkinson, was one of the principal troublemakers. Because of Wilkinson's indiscretion, the plot was prematurely revealed.

By this period of the war Wilkinson had risen to the rank of colonel and was serving in the north as an aide to General Gates. One day, shortly before the victory at Saratoga, General Conway sent an ill-advised letter to Gates in which he disclosed the nature and aims of the conspirators in full detail. Gates read the letter with satisfaction. He long had considered himself the finest general in the country and saw no reason why he should not replace Washington at the head of the armed forces. Having read Conway's letter, he showed it to his confidant, burly young Colonel Wilkinson.

A few days later, Gates sent Wilkinson south to Pennsylvania with a message for the Congress announcing his victory over General Burgoyne. During this trip, the convivial Wilkinson paid a visit to Washington's southern encampment. One night, he went to a neighboring tavern with Major McWilliams, an officer serving on the staff of General Stirling.

The two officers drank several tankards of ale together and discussed military and political questions. The more Wilkinson drank, the more freely his tongue wagged. He grew expansive, and to impress his friend the major, he began to boast of his inside knowledge of important affairs—of George Washington's imminent dismissal from the service, for example, and of the letter which General Conway had written to General Gates.

When Major McWilliams, in dismay, returned to camp·that night, he informed his commanding officer, General Stirling, of the conversation and of Conway's letter to Gates. Stirling, equally dismayed, promptly reported the entire affair to Washington.

The Commander in Chief wrote to Gates. He did not reveal that Wilkinson was the original source of his information, but he described Conway's letter in sufficient detail to convince the horrified Gates that a copy of the incriminating document had fallen into Washington's hands.

By the time Gates received Washington's letter, Wilkinson—now appointed a general by an act of Congress as a reward for delivering news of the Saratoga victory—had returned to the northern camp. As Gates read Washington's letter he was overcome with fear. How much of the plot was known? he howled. And who had betrayed him? Then he remembered that Washington's most trusted aide, Alexander Hamilton, had been in the camp only a few days after Conway's letter had arrived. Gates shouted to Wilkinson, "I have had a spy in my camp. . . . Colonel Hamilton has been sent up to me by General Washington, and, would you believe it, he purloined the copy of the letter out of that closet!"

Wilkinson, relieved to find that Gates did not suspect the real source of the leak, looked greatly astonished, and said nothing.

Gates then thought back to the day of Hamilton's visit. Yes, he was absolutely certain the culprit was Hamilton.

"The family being called out on business," he told Wilkinson, "he [Hamilton] was left alone an hour in this room, during which time he took Conway's letter out of that closet, and copied it, and the copy has been furnished to Washington!"

Wilkinson still did not disclose his role as the betrayer of Gates and Conway. But he did see an opportunity to discredit Colonel Robert Troup, a fellow officer on Gates' staff whom he especially disliked.

Colonel Troup, as Wilkinson knew, was a friend of both Burr and Hamilton. More important, he had been Hamilton's roommate at King's College in New York several years before. Wilkinson reminded Gates of Troup's friendship with Hamilton; then he insinuated that perhaps Troup, without meaning to, had revealed the contents of the letter to Hamilton.

Gates may have believed Wilkinson's story—but not for long. The truth soon reached him—that it was Wilkinson who had ruined everything by his drunken babbling.

In an angry note to Wilkinson, Gates said, "I am astonished if you really gave Major McWilliams such information, how you could *intimate* to me, that it was *possible* Colonel Troup *had conversed* with Colonel Hamilton upon the subject of Conway's letter."

Discovered at last by his superior officer, Wilkinson did not repent, nor beg forgiveness, nor even admit his indiscretion. Instead, he pretended to fly into a rage, claimed that his honor had been impugned—and challenged the Hero of Saratoga to a duel.

As they began to scurry for cover and to quarrel among themselves, the plotters came to resemble a group of road company actors playing in a third-rate farce. Gates flatly refused to fight the duel with Wilkinson. Instead he decided to discredit him, and to try to restore himself in Washington's favor at the same time.

He wrote a fawning and patently insincere letter to Washington in which he blamed Wilkinson for everything. It had been Wilkinson, he said, who had tried to put suspicion on Troup and Hamilton, in order to escape suspicion himself. "I did not listen to this insinuation against your aide or mine," Gates told the Commander in Chief. "I considered it even as ungenerous." In point of fact, he went on to explain to Washington, the entire affair was a plot of Wilkinson's. His aide had *forged* the letter from Conway in order to discredit both Conway and himself, Gates, with their respected and admired Commander in Chief.

By then Washington was satisfied to let the matter rest. The conspiracy had been revealed before it was ripe; the conspirators had been exposed, and when some of their explanations and self-justifications were published, they began to look ridiculous. Horatio

Gates would remain in the north, where his popularity made it inadvisable to replace him. But he would not take command of the Continental Army, and he would find it considerably harder to commit any serious mischief in the future.

Wilkinson did not escape so easily. He was placed under great pressure to resign, and did so before many weeks had passed. But he was not a man who could be kept down long. He had influential friends in Congress and in several of the states. Through them he set about to recoup his fortunes.

The next summer Congress appointed James Wilkinson to a new post. He was named Clothier-General to the Army, an ideal position if a man wanted to improve his own financial standing at the expense of the troops. And that, without doubt, was exactly what James Wilkinson did for the next several years.

11.

From Valley Forge to Monmouth

IN DECEMBER, 1777, Colonel Aaron Burr brought Malcolm's Regiment into winter quarters at Valley Forge where he and his men spent the darkest months of the war. The snowy encampment was a cold, dismal, windswept place. Food, shoes, blankets, medicine, everything the soldiers needed for health and comfort, were in short supply. In neighboring Lancaster the members of Congress quarreled among themselves, criticized Washington's conduct of the war, and refused his never-ending requests for the money with which to purchase necessities for his sick and hungry troops.

Before many weeks had passed at Valley Forge, young Colonel Burr had found another grievance to hold against his Commander in Chief. Bored and idle, he devised a plan to raid British outposts on Staten Island. He was thoroughly familiar with the area, he told Washington, and was on friendly terms with many of the inhabitants there. As a boy, sailing his boat from Elizabethtown, he often had landed across the water. Now he proposed to do so again, using 200 picked men from Malcolm's Regiment to form his party of hit-and-run marauders.

The general listened to Burr's plan, and then rejected it. This was bad enough. But several weeks later, when Washington allowed another officer to attempt a similar operation and the force was repulsed with heavy losses, Burr felt that Washington had used him badly. He believed that once again, for personal reasons, he had been kept from showing initiative and exercising authority.

Seething with discontent, Burr still managed to distinguish himself at Valley Forge when he was given a different—and rather unusual—assignment. At the time there was an unruly detachment of local militia stationed a few miles from the main camp near a strategic pass called "The Gulf." This detachment was supposed to guard the pass and raise the alarm if the enemy was seen approaching. When none of the enemy appeared, however, the soldiers grew tired of their seemingly pointless duty. They decided to provide themselves with some entertainment at the expense of the Continental troops in the main camp.

One night they raised the alarm, even though there was no enemy about, and then listened with glee as the entire army tumbled out of tents and huts.

The militia at The Gulf enjoyed the performance so much that the following night the alarm was raised again. And the next night, and the next.

To bring a halt to this unmilitary state of affairs, General Alexander McDougall asked for the services of Aaron Burr. Washington, who appreciated many of Burr's soldierly qualities even though he mistrusted his character, readily agreed to have Burr placed on temporary duty as commanding officer of the troublesome militia detachment.

Burr immediately showed his new command that he was not an officer who would tolerate any nonsense. He drilled the men from dawn till dark; he led them on a series of forced marches from one part of the encampment to another. Then, when they thought surely they were going to be allowed to rest, he ordered them into ranks and marched them back again. He visited the guard posts at any and every hour of the night so that the soldiers on duty there never knew when to expect him. He drove the detachment so relentlessly that most of the men, unaccustomed to the rigors of regular army training, came to hate their brisk, efficient commanding officer. They knew that one day he would have to return to his own regiment, but when would that blessed day come? A few of the more rebellious members of the detachment decided that they could not endure Colonel Burr any longer. They had to get rid of him—and the best way to do it, they agreed, was to murder him.

But Burr, alert to whatever schemes and plots might be afoot, soon got wind of their plans. Instead of reporting his discovery to higher authorities, as he should have done, he kept the information to himself. Then he prepared to smash the mutiny before it could make further headway.

His first step was to enter the guardroom and secretly remove the bullets from every musket in the detachment. His second step was to fall the men out for retreat, as though he suspected nothing.

Alone and erect, Burr walked slowly between the drawn-up ranks of mutinous soldiers, his unsheathed sword held firmly in his hand. All at once, as he passed in front of one of the ringleaders, the man leapt forward and shouted loudly, "Now is your time, boys!" He aimed his musket at Burr's head and pulled the trigger.

At the same moment Burr lifted his sword, then brought it down on the man's arm, striking with such force that he very nearly severed the arm in two. The act was coldhearted, but effective. The mutiny ended on the spot. After that there were no more problems of discipline in the detachment and no more false alarms to arouse the weary, half-starved Continentals in the main encampment.

Early in 1778, when American hopes were at an ebb, an event took place in France which was to have a decisive effect on the outcome of the war. For several years Louis XVI and his ministers had wished to strike a blow against their enemy, Great Britain, by openly supporting the American cause, but they didn't know whether it would be wise to do so.

Certainly, if the rebellious colonists had no real chance to win their independence, it would be foolhardy for France to rush to their aid. On the other hand, if the colonists *did* have a chance to win the conflict, then French assistance should be sent at once.

The news of the victory at Saratoga and the surrender of General Burgoyne's army provided the signal for which the French Government had been waiting. The American cause not only was just—it had a chance to succeed. On February 6, 1778, the American envoy in France, Benjamin Franklin, and French Foreign Minister Charles Vergennes signed a treaty of alliance for their countries. At last, after three years of isolation and struggle, the American nation had a strong and open ally.

British strategy now had to be adjusted to a new and powerful enemy. By the spring of 1778, plans had been made to evacuate Philadelphia and concentrate all available forces in New York City.

Prior to this time, the British fleet had remained in almost complete control of the Atlantic sea lanes and America's coastal waters. But in 1778 the French fleet posed a threat to British naval supremacy. Therefore, it was considered a safer plan to march overland from Philadelphia to New York rather than to risk a long and roundabout journey by water. Accordingly, in the middle of June the British commander, General Henry Clinton, who had succeeded General Howe only a few weeks before, led his army from the capital and began to march northeast across the flatlands of New Jersey.

Washington set out at once to pursue, shadow and harass Clinton, whose columns were swelled by 1,500 wagons and carts and by numerous private carriages bearing several thousand unhappy Tory citizens who had been afraid to be left in Philadelphia.

Neither the British nor the Americans were able to advance quickly on the march. Soaking rains were followed by periods of blazing sunshine that failed to dispel the humidity. The heat grew more intense. The temperature soared above a hundred degrees day after day, and the entire countryside sweltered in the grip of a heat wave. The soldiers of both armies, with their heavy field packs and rough woolen uniforms, suffered terrible agonies along the roads.

At last, on June 28th, Washington's forces caught up with the retiring enemy at Monmouth. An attack was begun with the hope it would end in a smashing American victory. Then, at a crucial moment in the battle, General Charles Lee, one of the American field commanders, did an incomprehensible thing: he ordered his 5,000 troops to retreat at the moment when they should have been advancing. Soon the confused men were fleeing headlong—without a single enemy soldier in sight.

The entire situation had suddenly changed. Instead of destroying the enemy, and perhaps bringing about an early armistice and an end to the war, the American army found itself in a desperate struggle to escape annihilation. Only Washington's timely appearance along the line of retreat, his rallying of the fleeing men, and his able generalship for the remainder of the afternoon helped to stabilize the fighting and bring the battle to an inconclusive close. By then, however, the chance for a total victory over Clinton and a quick end to hostilities was irretrievably lost.

General Lee's conduct at Monmouth was never satisfactorily explained. Perhaps he was a traitor in the pay of the enemy. Or perhaps, as some of his fellow officers concluded, he was merely an incomparable bungler, whose single error added months or even years to the length of the Revolutionary War.

12.

The "Westchester Lines"

PRECEDING THE Battle of Monmouth and during the battle itself, Aaron Burr finally overtaxed his strength and brought on a renewal of the illness that was to trouble him for the next five years.

Several days before the battle, he found himself in command of an entire brigade. His troops consisted of the men of Malcolm's Regiment and elements of two other regiments as well. From the time he assumed command, he slept very little. Despite the extraordinary heat and high humidity, which continued without letup, he insisted on exerting himself even more than usual in an effort to prepare his troops for battle.

On the eve of the fighting he scarcely paused to eat or rest. On the day of the battle he was continuously in action from sunup until several hours after dark. He led a number of charges, had his horse killed by a musket ball, and was pitched headfirst to the ground. Uninjured, he mounted another horse and rode back to rejoin the fighting. Toward midnight, when the last of the engagement was over, he threw himself down, completely exhausted, and fell asleep.

The next day he began to suffer acutely from an intestinal disorder which he had experienced in a less severe form once or twice before. Despite the pain, he was determined to remain on active duty as long as possible. During the summer months, when Washington asked him to undertake several arduous missions as an intelligence officer, he performed them promptly and without complaint.

In the autumn, though, his condition grew considerably worse. He requested a leave of absence and, returning to Elizabethtown, spent several weeks among the relatives and neighbors whom he had known during his childhood. This brief rest in Elizabethtown had a good effect on his general health, but he continued to suffer from the intestinal condition. A doctor in the village told him that only an extensive convalescence could accomplish a complete cure.

By then his leave was up, and he rode to duty at West Point. For a few weeks he served as commandant of that vital fortress.

After Christmas, Burr was given his last and most responsible assignment. On January 13, 1779, he took command of a wide area called the "Westchester Lines," which lay between the American army posts in Westchester County, New York, and the British army posts at Kingsbridge, some twenty miles to the south.

Lawlessness was commonplace inside the Westchester Lines, and robbery, assault and even murder were far from exceptional occurrences. Local cut-throats made it a regular practice to plunder law-abiding citizens. Tory attacked Patriot, and Patriot returned the compliment by attacking Tory.

Almost the worst culprits of all were the American soldiers stationed in the area. The first day Burr spent at his new headquarters at White Plains he saw an army detachment return from an overnight "scouting expedition." The returning soldiers staggered under the weight of grandfather clocks, silverware, crockery, glassware, blankets and clothing—all stolen from hapless American families whom they were supposed to protect.

Burr soon began to alter things. He forced his men to end their looting. He established discipline among them, and demanded a decent standard of conduct. He reestablished their pride in themselves as soldiers, made a fighting force of them, and led them to victory over a strong British raiding party in a sharp engagement.

With disciplined soldiers at his command, and with the British driven back to their forts at Kingsbridge, he was able to put an end to the violence and civil bloodshed which long had plagued that part of the countryside. In all, he was in command of the Westchester Lines for little more than two months, yet in that short space of time he managed to change conditions throughout the area to a remarkable degree.

A citizen named Samuel Young lived within the lines during the war. Afterward, he wrote an account of Burr's accomplishments.

The troops of which [Burr] took command were, at the time . . . undisciplined, negligent and discontented. In a few days these very men were transformed into brave and honest defenders; orderly and cheerful, confident in their own courage, and loving to adoration their commander, whom every man considered as his personal friend. . . . During the whole of his command there was not a single desertion, not a single death by sickness, not one soldier made prisoner by the enemy. . . . After the first ten days there was not a single instance of robbery. The whole country under his command enjoyed security. . . . Colonel Simcoe, one of the most daring and active partisans in the British army, was . . . opposed to Burr on the lines, yet . . . [he was] completely held in check. But perhaps the highest eulogy on Colonel Burr is, that [after he departed] no man could be found capable of executing his plans, though the example was before them. When Burr left the lines a sadness spread over the country, and the most gloomy forebodings were too soon fulfilled.

General McDougall's adjutant general, Richard Platt, visited the area during the winter of 1779. He, too, described the effect of Burr's presence on the lines. The officers, soldiers and inhabitants "were inspired with confidence by a system of consummate skill, astonishing vigilance, and extreme activity, which, in a like manner, made such an impression on the enemy, that after an unsuccessful attack on one of [Burr's] advance posts, he never made any other attack on our lines during the winter. [Burr's] humanity, and constant regard to keep the security of the property and persons of the inhabitants from injury and insult, were not less conspicuous than his military skill. No man was insulted or disturbed. . . . A country, which for three years before had been a scene of robbery, cruelty, and murder, became at once the abode of security and peace."

But the ceaseless efforts which Burr was compelled to exert to reform his own soldiers, quell the lawlessness of private citizens, and prevent the incursions of the enemy completely ruined his health. On March 10, 1779, he submitted his resignation to General Washington, who accepted it shortly afterward with sincere regret.

Although he was still only twenty-three, Burr had been a soldier on active duty for four years. During this time he had taken part in numerous battles and campaigns, and had served with distinction both as a staff officer and as a commander in the field. His reputation for courage was unquestioned; his name was known and honored in Patriot circles everywhere for the part he had played on the Wilderness March, in the Jersey campaigns, on Long Island, in Westchester.

Burr himself never looked back on his military career with anything but pride and satisfaction. Although he had spent four precious years in his country's service, and had temporarily lost his health as well, he never spoke with regret about that period of his life.

He had craved martial distinction—and had achieved it. He had suffered physical hardship—and had endured it. He had faced danger and death—and had met them with calmness and resolution. Surely he was entitled to believe that his own character had been strengthened by four years of responsibility, self-discipline and devotion to duty.

Yet, paradoxically, his character had been weakened, too. Few men have understood Burr as well as James Parton, who wrote a biography of him, more than a hundred years ago. Parton pointed out that for one thing, Burr had become a spendthrift while in the army. Parton wrote:

During the four years of [Burr's] connection with the army, his fortune was greatly impaired. . . . He had the popular and fatal vice of improvidence. . . . With amazing talents for gaining money, he had an equally wonderful facility for getting rid of it. It slipped through his fingers; it ran out of his pocket; it would *not* stay with him. To see a fellow soldier in distress, and to empty his purse for his relief were simultaneous actions with him.

Nor did he spare expense in forwarding any scheme of his own, whether of pleasure or advantage. From his own correspondence . . . it is plain he was a frequent lender of money to embarrassed friends . . . it is pleasant . . . enough while the money lasts; but it never does last. No fortune can stand the strain of uncalculating improvidence. And a worse feature of the case is, that a man who is careless of [what is his] is in frightful danger of losing some portion of his regard for [what is yours] also. . . .

But, as Parton indicated, there were more serious dangers.

Another tendency of [Burr's] nature was strengthened by the war. It is the soldier's art to constantly adapt means to ends; it is his duty, by all means, to gain his ends. His object, the destruction of the enemy, is simple, obvious, unmistakable; and, in encompassing it, he not merely *may,* but *must,* be deaf to the cry of anguish. He is not merely released from the moral restraints of peace, but is obliged to trample them under foot. He destroys without compunction; he kills without compassion. His mind is fixed upon his *object;* he burns merely to *succeed.* Victory alone, victory always, is accepted as proof of his ability. But in peace it is not always glorious to succeed; for then, we estimate success chiefly by the means used to attain it.

Aaron Burr . . . was a man who had by nature a marvelous faculty of bringing things to pass. He saw his *object* with eagle clearness and he had a wonderfully intuitive sense of the means, and all the means, and particularly the *readiest* means, by which that object could be reached . . . four years of a soldier's life may have had the two-fold effect, first of intensifying his perception of objects to be gained, and secondly, of diminishing his scrupulousness with regard to the use of the means [for gaining those ends].

At the age of twenty-three, when he returned to civilian life, Aaron Burr was an ex-war hero, with a dissipated fortune and a growing appetite for elegant surroundings and lavish expenditures. He was also a young man who had discovered that to achieve one's ambitions one may occasionally be forced to act unscrupulously. Of almost all the lessons in the world, this was probably the most dangerous he could have learned.

13.

Death and Treason

ARON BURR'S return to civilian life was not a happy one. Ill health continued to trouble him. In order to reduce the chronic pain caused by his condition he was forced to follow a strict diet, avoiding rich food and wine.

His physical strength declined, and so did his mental exertions. He began to study law again, but made little progress. To divert himself, he leafed through a variety of political tracts and philosophical essays, but when he did his attention wandered, and he would put the volume aside and fall into a gloomy trance.

His mind was as troubled as his body. Inertia gripped him. His powers of concentration seemed to have been destroyed, and life appeared to have no purpose.

Only once, for a day or two, was there an interruption in his tedious existence. While he was visiting friends in New Haven, Connecticut, a British raiding party landed on the nearby coast. Soon the alarm was raised, and the entire countryside took fright at the news that ex-Governor Tryon of New York, a fierce Tory, was approaching at the head of 3,000 troops. His men had sacked and burned a village to the east, and in an hour or two the same treatment would be dealt out to New Haven.

Lying in bed, where he had gone to rest, Burr heard the cries of the people rushing about outside his window and the boom of a cannon being fired in the distance. He leapt out of bed, dressed quickly, and ran into the street. He shouted that he would lead the local militia against the invaders, but many of the militia already had scattered to their homes and there seemed to be no way to defend the village.

Then Burr learned that not far off, on the campus of Yale College, the students were attempting to organize themselves to fight against Governor Tryon's raiders. Burr found a horse and galloped to the college yard, where he told the students who he was. They raised a loud cheer and placed themselves at once under the command of the renowned Colonel Burr. As he began to form them into squads and companies, some members of the militia, shamed by the courage of the young college boys, approached the yard and volunteered their services. Soon the little force was divided into several companies—and Colonel Burr led his men into battle for the last time.

The engagement was brief. Burr and his students were greatly outnumbered. They attacked the British left flank and forced the enemy to halt and take cover.

Finally Tryon, bringing up reinforcements and cannon, drove the Americans in good order back through the town. Before the British departed and returned to their ships, they burned New Haven and robbed many of its inhabitants of their possessions. But Burr's band of college boys at least had the comfort of knowing that they had done their best and had made things as difficult as possible for the raiders.

For Burr it was only a temporary diversion, however. Soon he was sunk in gloom again. He remained idly at his lawbooks, ate sparingly, and, when he wrote to his friends, confessed there were times when he was not "always" in a cheerful frame of mind.

But he revealed to no one what was troubling him more than anything else: The present seemed dark because the future seemed darker. He was in love—desperately—with a married woman, and he had no reason whatsoever to hope that one day he might make her his wife.

He had not lost touch with Theodosia Prevost. They exchanged letters often, and she implicitly acknowledged that if only circumstances *had* been different, he would have been welcome as a suitor. But she was a lady of good family, with a proper regard for the social proprieties and her own reputation. Though her husband was absent, he was still her husband. Though her love for Colonel Prevost, and his love for her, might long since have died, as long as she *was* his wife she could accept no improper attentions from another man, nor would she conduct herself in any way that might stain her honor. She would write to young Colonel Burr as often as he wished, she would encourage his friendship—but she would offer him nothing more.

Burr fretted and thought glumly of the future. He took an interest in Theodosia's affairs. He did what he could to keep her Patriot neighbors from persecuting her because her husband was an English soldier and she therefore was suspected of being a Tory.

Burr wrote his friends on her behalf and prevented her house and other property from being seized. He wrote to Theodosia, but he did not describe his moods of depression nor the strength of his feelings. And he did not visit her in New Jersey. He was afraid that if he did, he might lose his self-control and speak of his love. That, he feared, would so displease her that she would put an end to their correspondence. Therefore he remained away, nursed his ill health, and passed the idle hours as best he could.

Then, early in 1780, he learned that Colonel Prevost had fallen sick and died while serving in the West Indies. In a moment everything was changed. Burr's lethargy vanished. It wasn't long before he was saddling his horse and riding away to Paramus to visit and console the colonel's widow.

Although he now became a frequent visitor at the home of Theodosia, their courtship did not proceed as swiftly as Burr might have hoped. There were a number of reasons for this. One was simple propriety. Social convention, if nothing else, demanded that a decent amount of time should elapse between the death of Colonel Prevost and any announcement by his widow that she intended to marry again. Also, Theodosia may have felt far from certain that she really *did* want to remarry, and even if she did, there still was no compelling reason for her to hasten her decision.

Other impediments stood in Burr's way. His health had improved, but he was not yet well. His funds were low and he certainly did not possess enough money to support a wife and perhaps several of her children. In order to do that, he first had to complete the legal studies which he had scarcely begun, and then obtain a license to practice as an attorney. So he and Theodosia postponed any final decision. But they continued to correspond, and Burr appeared, whenever his health permitted, as a guest in the Prevost house in Paramus.

During one of his visits to Paramus he witnessed an unforgettable scene and learned in detail how his former commanding officer, Benedict Arnold, had been guilty of treason. Burr was sitting in Theodosia Prevost's parlor one evening when they heard the sound of approaching horses. A few minutes later a young woman in riding clothes, her face covered by a veil, burst into the room. She hurried toward Mrs. Prevost and was about to speak, when she glimpsed Burr in the shadows.

"Am I safe?" she asked Mrs. Prevost. "Is this gentleman a friend?"

"Oh yes," Theodosia replied, "he is my most particular friend, Colonel Burr."

"Thank God!" the woman said. "I've been playing the hypocrite, and I'm tired of it."

She removed her veil, and they recognized at once that she was Benedict Arnold's wife. Before her marriage she had been Peggy Shippen. She and Burr had

known one another all their lives. When Burr and his
sister Sally had been sent as small orphaned children
to Philadelphia to escape the smallpox epidemic rag-
ing in Princeton they had been taken to Peggy Shippen's house.

Now Burr listened as the almost hysterical Peggy
Arnold told them how she had just come from West
Point. There she had deceived Washington, Alexander Hamilton and the rest of the general's staff in
order to keep herself from being arrested. As she
talked, the real story of her husband's treason came
out.

By then it was known that Benedict Arnold had
been a traitor, but no suspicion had attached to his
pretty young wife. Everyone believed she was innocent
and felt great pity for her—a pity entirely misplaced.
She was equally guilty, Peggy Arnold told Burr and
Mrs. Prevost that night. She had urged her husband to
betray his country and accept money from the British.
She herself had conducted some of the negotiations,
had arranged for her husband, the commanding officer
at West Point, to deliver the plans of the fort and, if
possible, even the fort itself into the hands of the enemy.

Burr kept her secret, never revealing what she had
said until her role in the treasonous plot had become
known and the information no longer could be used
against her.

The next day Peggy Arnold resumed her journey.
As he watched her ride away, Burr may have remembered his own estimate of Arnold, made just after the
wilderness march was over. "Arnold," he had said, ". . .
has not a particle of moral courage. He is utterly

unprincipled, and has no love of country or self-respect to guide him. He is not to be trusted anywhere but under the eye of a superior. . . ."

How accurate his estimate of Benedict Arnold had been! And even more curious, how much of that same estimate would one day be applied against himself, when—like Arnold—he had accumulated a number of large debts which he could not readily meet and when —like Arnold—he had lost the patriotic zeal which had made him such an excellent soldier.

14.

"An Open Countenance—Thoughts Closely Concealed"

URING THE following months Burr gradually recovered his health. At the same time his spirits and mental energy began to revive. He visited Paramus whenever he could and continued to interest himself in Theodosia Prevost's affairs. On one occasion he provided sixty pounds to hire a tutor for her sons, John and Augustin Prevost, though by that time he had almost nothing left of his inheritance and was growing acutely short of funds.

Lack of money drove him to renew his legal studies, but at first he didn't make rapid progress. He became a student of William Patterson, a friend from his Princeton days, who already had become a lawyer. Patterson, a methodical young man, believed that every law student should devote at least two or three years to the study of legal theory before turning to the more practical aspects of the profession. After several months Burr decided that this would never do for *him.* He didn't have that much time to spare. So he parted from Patterson and began to study with Thomas Smith, a former New York City attorney, who had moved to Haverstraw to avoid living under the British occupation.

Thomas Smith did not think that a student had to spend several years absorbing legal theory unless he cared to. He let Burr devise his own course of study. Using a system of questions and answers, the impatient young student soon found that he was preparing himself for the bar at a much brisker pace than he ever could have done under the more conventional methods of Patterson.

Several fresh considerations now encouraged Burr to complete his studies as quickly as possible. Chief among them was the understanding he reached with Theodosia Prevost. She agreed to marry him as soon as he passed his examinations and had a reasonable prospect of being able to support himself and his family by the practice of law.

Public events also drove Burr forward with greater haste and energy. On October 19, 1781, a large British army under General Cornwallis surrendered at Yorktown, Virginia. After this decisive defeat of the enemy, it was clear the War of Independence was virtually over. From that day on it was merely a question of time before the Confederation of thirteen states and Great Britain signed a treaty ending hostilities, and a new era of peace began in America. With peace would come a settled way of life—and the chance for a young man to get on in the world.

Another public event made haste even more imperative. At almost the same time that Cornwallis was offering to surrender his troops at Yorktown, a bill was introduced into the New York Legislature to bar all Tory lawyers from future practice. The bill was certain to be enacted, and when it was—since most prominent New York lawyers *were* Tories—the effect would be tremendous. As soon as the British troops evacuated New York a flood of cases would arise, but there would be hardly any licensed attorneys to accept them. At that moment a young lawyer would find himself with the opportunity to acquire clients and climb swiftly to professional eminence. It was an opportunity that would never occur again, and Burr had no intention of allowing it to slip by.

Aaron Burr worked feverishly, eighteen and twenty hours a day, preparing for his examinations. He was too busy to visit Paramus now, but he did manage to carry on a regular correspondence with Theodosia.

The letters they exchanged were not those of conventional lovers. Instead of romantic and passionate avowals of affection, they sent one another cool, reasoned intellectual documents. Instead of describing the depths of their ardor, or lamenting the wretchedness they felt at their enforced separation, they discussed authors like Jean Jacques Rousseau and Lord Chesterfield, whose educational theories interested them.

On the subject of Lord Chesterfield they were not in agreement. Theodosia believed that the titled Englishman exhibited certain grave moral faults, and of these she did not approve.

"The indulgence you applaud in Chesterfield," she wrote to Burr, "is the only part of his writings I think reprehensible. . . . 'The weakness of humanity' is an easy apology [for such conduct]; or rather, a license to practice intemperance; and it is particularly agreeable and flattering to such practitioners, as it brings the most virtuous on a level with the most vicious."

Burr, however, was not to be dissuaded from his admiration of Chesterfield. Few writers appealed to him so greatly, and no writer offered him so congenial a point of view. It would be no exaggeration to say that in many ways Burr actually began to pattern himself on Chesterfield, that he adopted his ideals with all their defects, and that he found the English nobleman's worldly advice extremely serviceable in the conduct of his own affairs.

And what exactly *were* the ideals of the fourth Earl of Chesterfield, as expressed in his famous *Letters* to his son? What advice did he offer Philip Stanhope, whom he wished to educate for the career of a courtier?

The ideals were a curious blend of the thoroughly acceptable and the thoroughly despicable. The advice offered was "practical," cynical and—unhappily for poor Philip Stanhope—utterly interminable as well.

In letter after letter, Lord Chesterfield poured out his "wisdom" for the benefit of the young boy he hoped to form into an urbane, witty, self-serving "gentleman." Sometimes his advice must have appealed to Burr because it seemed novel and clever, sometimes because Burr already had discovered for himself the usefulness of similar ideas.

The two men were amazingly alike in outlook and temperament. Burr believed that a gentleman never lost his self-possession in public, and so did Chesterfield. Burr was ambitious and craved public acclaim. So did the Earl. Both men held their fellow creatures in contempt, yet neither saw the inconsistency in their wish to be esteemed by the very men whom they despised.

In fairness to Chesterfield, it must be said that some of his beliefs were those of an upright man. "I call corruption," he wrote, "the taking of a sixpence more than the just and known salary of your employment, under any pretence whatever." No doubt the Earl was right: if you are a public official, you should not accept bribes. The only trouble was that he saw nothing wrong in attempting to bribe other officials, and later in life expressed his grief that he had not been able to purchase a seat in Parliament for his son for the sum of 2,500 pounds.

The Earl's advice to Philip Stanhope covered many aspects of private and public life. A boy like his son, he was sure, would have to work with extreme diligence if he were to get on in the world—and nothing was more important to Chesterfield than "getting on."

"Six, or at the most seven hours' sleep," he told Philip, "is . . . as much as you or anybody can want. . . . More is only laziness and dozing; and is, I am persuaded, both unwholesome and stupefying. . . . I have often gone to bed at six in the morning, and rose, notwithstanding, at eight; by which means I got many hours in the morning, that my companions lost. . . . Know the true value of time, snatch, seize, and enjoy every moment of it. No idleness, no laziness, no procrastination."

Then, according to the Earl, his son should be careful to cultivate good manners, for "nobody was ever loved who was not well-bred." A curious idea—but one in which Burr, with his own polished manners, probably believed implicitly.

After that there was more about getting on in the world. How did one do it? Men, whom one despised, were to be flattered. Women, whom one despised, were to be flattered, and if they were attractive enough, were to be seduced as well. "Every man is to be had one way or another, and every woman almost any way." For "every woman is infallibly to be gained by every sort of flattery, and every man by one sort or another."

And then there was one final lesson that had to be learned if one were to prosper in this cynical, cold-hearted world. Be secretive. Chesterfield wrote this bit of advice in Italian: *"Volto sciolto, pensieri stretti"*— "An open countenance, thoughts closely concealed." How familiar this idea must have seemed to Burr, the youthful employer of codes and ciphers, the matchless intelligence officer and employer of spies, the cool young man who already had made a lifelong habit of concealment. No wonder that Theodosia Prevost felt an instinctive uneasiness about Lord Chesterfield's *Letters*—and no wonder that Burr found their contents so congenial.

While Burr and Theodosia exchanged opinions, he faithfully followed the Earl's advice: "No idleness, no laziness, no procrastination." From sunup till long after dark he worked at his lawbooks. And at last the time came when he knew he was ready to take his examinations.

Before he could take them, however, he had to overcome one more difficulty. In New York State there was a fixed rule that every candidate had to study at least three years with a qualified teacher before he could take his examinations for the bar. Burr had studied only six months with Thomas Smith, and knew he would be disqualified unless he could circumvent the rule.

The Supreme Court of New York would decide on his plea to have the rule set aside. The court consisted of three judges, and Burr started out to gain their favor.

First, he supplied Theodosia with a number of arguments and had her approach Judge Hobard, who was a friend of hers. They won Judge Hobard's unofficial approval. Next, Burr talked with Judge Yates, whom he already knew. Judge Yates also indicated his unofficial approval.

Then Burr rode quickly to Albany to present his petition to Chief Justice Richard Morris. Burr offered Morris several letters of introduction, including one from his former superior officer in the Continental Army, General Alexander McDougall. Burr also wrote a letter of his own to the Chief Justice, explaining what he believed were the special circumstances which governed his case.

Burr explained that he had discovered "a rule of unexpected rigor, which, if strictly adhered to, must effectually exclude me from this bar. Mr. Judge Yates gives me reason to hope this rule may be enlarged. If it should be deemed unadvisable to make [an enlargement] of such latitude as may include me within a general description, perhaps my particular situation may be thought to claim particular indulgence."

Burr then went on to offer some arguments which, typically enough, were extremely ingenious, though not entirely truthful or valid.

"Before the revolution," Burr wrote, "and long before the existence of the present rule, I had served some time with an attorney of another state. At that period I could have availed myself of this service; and, surely, no rule could be intended . . . to injure one *whose only misfortune is having sacrificed his time, his constitution, and his fortune, to his country.*"

When Burr claimed a special dispensation on the grounds of patriotism, he was justified. But when he claimed that his desultory legal studies in 1775 with Tappan Reeve in Litchfield had actually qualified him for the right to a bar examination, he was guilty of an ingenious and deliberate lie.

The court delayed consideration of Burr's case for several exasperating weeks. When the judges announced they would hear it, Burr could not find a single lawyer in Albany who would offer his petition. He had no alternative but to offer it himself.

He pleaded his own case with the clarity and brevity which were to become his professional hallmark and won the court's approval of his major point. Because of his military service, the judges decided that the ordinary three-year period of study would be waived. He could take the New York bar examinations, but would receive no special consideration; he would have to prove his qualifications like any other candidate.

The last barrier had fallen. Burr took his examinations shortly afterward and passed them easily. On January 19, 1782, he received his license as an attorney, and on April 17th was admitted to practice in New York State.

There was a last flurry of letters, and then Burr rode south to Paramus.

On July 2, 1782, "Aaron Burr of the State of N. York, esquire, and Theodosia Prevost of Bergen County, State of N. Jersey," met before the Reverend David Bogart, and were soon "joined in lawful wedlock." Marriage and a new career now lay before the twenty-six-year-old Burr. Proud and ambitious though he was, he could not have foreseen the extent of his future success and how quickly he would achieve it.

15.

The Waiting Game

FOLLOWING THEIR MARRIAGE, Burr and Theodosia moved to Albany where he practiced law for a year, gaining a reputation as one of the most able attorneys in that part of the state.

In Albany the Burrs had the first of their two children, a baby girl. She was born June 21, 1783, and, at her father's insistence, was named Theodosia after her mother. Their other child, Sally, named after Burr's sister, was born two years later.

In November, 1783, the British army finally evacuated New York City. Burr, more eager than ever to seize the opportunity he had foreseen, soon moved there from Albany with his wife and child and opened a law office. Before many weeks had passed, his judgment was vindicated. He found himself with as many clients as he had anticipated, some men of considerable wealth whose patronage meant a succession of large legal fees.

Month by month his professional reputation grew. So did the amount of his income. At the age of thirty, Burr was earning at least $10,000 a year—in those days a very substantial sum—and all his financial difficulties should have been over.

They were, however, only destined to grow worse. By now the brilliant young attorney was an inveterate spendthrift, a man who could not put aside a penny of what he earned. He was forever living more sumptuously than he could afford to; he was forever spending more than he was taking in. For the sake of vanity and personal indulgence his parlor had to display the richest furnishings, his table the choicest foods and wines, his library the latest and most expensive books. Pride forced him to spend recklessly—and spend he did—so that little by little, during the days of his apparent prosperity, he was actually sliding deeper and deeper into debt.

After two or three years of married life, Burr's domestic happiness was marred by a shadow. His wife, Theodosia, fell sick, and the first symptoms of a serious illness began to appear. She suffered considerable pain; following each fresh attack, she was subject to fits of extreme depression. A number of doctors were able to provide superficial relief, but not a cure. Nobody realized at the time that her pain was caused by the cancer which eventually would kill her.

Burr had not been in New York more than a few months before he was faced with an important decision. He was approached by several prominent citizens, who pointed out he was a notable member of the community and it was his duty to stand for public office. Would he be willing to allow his name to be put in nomination for the New York State Assembly?

Burr hesitated. At this time he felt no interest in political affairs. He had a rapidly growing law practice and a wife and daughter with whom he wished to spend whatever hours he could spare from his work. Why seek public office? There was little money to be gained from it, and as yet, in 1784, very little prestige. To an opportunist like Burr, to a man with a "practical" turn of mind who was interested only in serving his own ends, a political career at this point did not offer an alluring prospect.

But the Assembly did meet in the city, and Burr knew that he might attend its gatherings without any great inconvenience to himself or harm to his law practice. Indeed, he would meet many of the leading men of the state, and some of them might become valuable clients in the future. So, with no great enthusiasm, he allowed his name to be put in nomination and in April, 1784, was duly elected a member of the State Assembly.

Burr served his term, and then returned to private practice. He had spent his first days in the political arena and, perhaps to his own surprise, had found the experience stimulating. To pass a bill by influencing the minds of other men, to exercise persuasion, to flatter, cajole, maneuver—didn't it really resemble the fighting of a battle? And didn't he have a conspicuous talent for waging such battles successfully?

Burr decided to wait on the sidelines, to study the political scene, and then to see if at some future time it might not pay him to run for office again. It was at this point, despite an initial reluctance, that political affairs began to absorb his interest. Eventually they came to dominate his life.

During the next four years Burr remained in the city and practiced law with gratifying success. At first he was only one of a handful of brilliant young attorneys who dominated the legal profession in New York. The others were his former army friends, Robert Troup, James Kent, Rufus King, John Jay, and Alexander Hamilton. But as time went by, it was increasingly acknowledged that two lawyers in the city outshone the rest—Burr and Hamilton.

On the surface, they seemed much alike. Each was short, spare, energetic, and carried himself with an easy and aristocratic grace. Each had the wit, good manners and eloquence to charm many women; each had the intelligence, self-possession and force of personality to impress other men.

In character they also appeared to resemble each other. Both were proud, ambitious, resourceful, and courageous. But there were also significant differences between them. Hamilton was generally open and frank; Burr habitually reserved and devious. Hamilton was a warmhearted and romantic idealist; Burr a clear-minded and cool-hearted cynic. Most important of all, Hamilton basically was a man of integrity, while Burr, despite his great intelligence and personal courage, would compromise principle if it served his ambition or pride.

The two acted very differently during the period

immediately following the end of the Revolutionary War. By 1785 it had become obvious to many leading citizens that America needed a new form of government. The old Confederation had outlived its usefulness. Grave problems faced the country, and the Continental Congress was unable to deal with them effectively.

Times were hard for many Americans. Thousands of farmers were in debt, with no hope of escaping their indebtedness. Thousands of Continental veterans were without jobs or money. Inflation hurt small tradesmen and members of the working classes. The weak national government was totally discredited and on the verge of bankruptcy. Business was poor in almost every section of the country, domestic manufacturing at a standstill, and foreign trade almost nonexistent. The fear of riot or insurrection was widespread. Each of the individual states threatened to solve its difficulties in its own way and, if necessary, was willing to secede from the Confederation. At any moment, the fabric of the nation seemed ready to rip into a hundred pieces.

During this crisis of American life, Hamilton, who had been born in the West Indies, felt a rising passion to serve his adopted country. He long had advocated the abandonment of the original Confederation and the transformation of the thirteen loosely connected states into a strong and vigorous Federal Republic. Now he began to devote his time and energy to that end.

Burr, though a native American, felt no such passion for service. He was content to let other men solve

America's problems, to let the Federalists and the anti-Federalists gather their forces for the titanic struggle ahead. Hamilton and James Madison of Virginia led their fellow delegates to Philadelphia for the great Constitutional Convention of 1786, and then continued to direct the fight for the acceptance of the Constitution until, in 1787, it was adopted by the necessary majority of states. While these climactic events were taking place, Aaron Burr remained in New York City, a private citizen, uncommitted to either side of the struggle. His interest in the Constitution was slight; his interest in his own affairs was all-consuming.

16.

A Political Coup

THE YEAR 1788 was not a joyful one for Aaron Burr. His family was reduced to three by the death of his younger daughter, Sally. Then his wife, Theodosia, began to lose the power of her limbs and no longer could walk upstairs without assistance. His debts were increasing, too. Despite a flourishing legal practice, he always seemed to owe money to someone—to tradesmen, doctors, business associates with whom he speculated and from whom he borrowed funds.

Yet Burr never considered the one course that many men would have taken. He gave no thought to the possibility of cutting his expenses. Retrench? *Colonel Burr* retrench? And admit to the world that he really could *not* afford to leave the perfectly comfortable house at 10 Little Queen Street for the more spacious quarters, complete with garden and grape arbor, which he had selected on Maiden Lane? Pride forbade such an admission, while arrogance prompted him to believe that a man of his industry, intelligence and shrewdness could somehow overcome the financial difficulties that beset him. A lucrative speculation, a killing in western lands or domestic bonds and—presto! —overnight the most tremendous debts would vanish, with enough left in hand for new entertainment and new display.

It was also in 1788, after three years of inactivity, that Burr resumed his political career. His first modest step seemed foolhardy. He let his name be placed in nomination for the State Assembly on the anti-Federalist ticket at a time when the Federalists controlled a large majority in the city.

The anti-Federalist slate of candidates had little chance of winning. But Burr, like most successful politicians, was a patient man. His eye was on the future. The loss of a single battle was unimportant; the winning of the war and the destruction of the enemy were what mattered.

When defeat came, he was neither surprised nor disappointed. Indeed, he had accomplished all that he had intended. By letting his name be placed in nomination he had shown a willingness to reenter public life and hold public office. One day a better opportunity would present itself, and then he would take the next step up the ladder.

Within a year his opportunity came. By that time the nation had elected George Washington its first President, and John Adams its first Vice-President; Senators and members of the House of Representatives also had been elected, and, in some states, a governor as well.

The Federalist Party was securely in power. The President, though not affiliated with either party, was politically conservative and favored the Federalist point of view. Adams, the Vice-President, was a Federalist from Massachusetts. The most influential member of the President's cabinet was the Secretary of the Treasury, Alexander Hamilton, the leader of the Federalist Party. The Federalists also held a majority in the Senate and the House of Representatives and in several of the various state legislatures.

There had been successful anti-Federalist candidates, too. One was New York's veteran politician and longtime governor, George Clinton. Tremendously popular within his own state, Clinton nevertheless had been unable to stop the Federalist tide single-handed. Now, faced with a Federalist majority in the state legislature and with political rivals entrenched in power, he began to search about for useful allies.

He soon sought out Aaron Burr. The important position of New York State Attorney General was vacant. Would Burr be interested in filling it—and, by accepting the favor, agree to an alliance with Clinton?

The decision was a vital one for Burr. The Attorney Generalship would bring him further prominence in New York. In addition, the support of Clinton would be invaluable for his political future. But the duties of office would consume much of his time; because he would have to reduce his law practice, his income would drop sharply. With debts ever increasing, such a drop would be most inconvenient. After hesitation, Burr decided the chance was too good to miss. In 1789 he became the Attorney General of New York and a person of considerable importance in local political circles.

Perhaps there was an additional motive behind Burr's acceptance of the post. At the time New York owned seven million acres of public land in the western part of the state. When Burr became Attorney General, he also became, by virtue of his office, a member of the State Land Commission. During his term the Commission approved the dispersement of more than five and a half million acres of the public lands, at an average price of one to three shillings an acre.

One sale created a scandal, and prompted a charge of bribery against Burr: the sale of over three and a half million acres—more than half the total acreage—to a single man, Alexander McComb, at a price of only eightpence an acre, or less than one-fourth the price paid by other purchasers. The implications were that Burr and his associates, already friendly to McComb, had let him make an extremely advantageous purchase and later had received a portion of the profits in a prearranged "under-the-table" deal.

The charge of bribery against Burr was never proved. Perhaps in this instance he was innocent. Nevertheless, two facts remain: he was a member of the Land Commission, and had accepted the Attorney Generalship—with a loss of personal income—only a short time before the purchase was arranged. Whether he was innocent or not, suspicions tarnished his reputation.

Not long afterward, a number of events occurred which even a man with Burr's political acumen could not have foreseen. Early in 1791, one of New York's two United States Senators, General Philip Schuyler, ran for reelection. He was a leading Federalist and the father-in-law of Alexander Hamilton.

At that time a senator was not elected by direct popular vote, but by the members of a state legislature. Since the New York State Legislature was strongly Federalist, it was an accepted conclusion that General Schuyler would be returned to office without difficulty, a victor over any candidate whom Governor Clinton and the anti-Federalists might offer in opposition.

Behind the scenes, however, some unusual factors were at work. The Federalists in New York were led at the time by two important and ambitious families, the Schuylers and the Livingstons. Two years before, Alexander Hamilton and the Schuylers had seriously offended the numerous members of the Livingston clan. They had supported Rufus King, only recently arrived in the state from Massachusetts, as the second senatorial candidate from New York, ignoring the pretensions and claims of their allies.

They also had offended the Livingstons in another matter. It had been assumed that Robert Livingston, the head of the family, would be appointed Chief Justice of the United States Supreme Court, an appointment appropriate to his age, abilities and importance.

But instead, another New York Federalist, young John Jay, had been designated Chief Justice through the influence and political manipulation of Hamilton.

Sensing the growing anger of the Livingstons, Governor Clinton cautiously approached them. Perhaps Burr was a party to the scheme. Certainly he was on friendly terms with several members of the family, particularly with Brockholst Livingston, who had been a classmate of his at Princeton.

Before the election an agreement was reached. The Livingstons, secretly combining with the forces of Clinton, would work to defeat the common enemy— Hamilton. But the Livingstons, still outwardly loyal to the Federalist cause, could not support a rabid anti-Federalist without giving the game away. The Livingstons and Clinton selected a compromise candidate —Aaron Burr.

Hamilton and his father-in-law, General Schuyler, had no inkling of the plot against them. With complete self-assurance they watched the proceedings begin in the state legislature.

General Schuyler's name was the only one placed in nomination. The voting started. To Hamilton and Schuyler's absolute incredulity, he was rejected. To their further disbelief and slowly rising fury, the name of Aaron Burr was then put forward and the voting resumed. Burr received a majority in both Houses— and became the new United States Senator from the State of New York.

The election was a tremendous triumph for Burr. At a single stroke he had gained national prominence, great personal power, and immense prestige. Ahead lay six years in the United States Senate and the chance ultimately to rise to undreamed-of heights.

But his election had another and less promising consequence. It secured for Burr the implacable hatred of the ambitious and immensely gifted Hamilton, "the Giant of the Federalists." Their rivalry began on the day of Burr's election and the defeat of General Schuyler. From that time forward the two men engaged in a long, violent and partisan struggle for power within New York State and the nation—a struggle that eventually would lead them to a dueling ground at Weehawken, New Jersey.

17.

Senator Burr

WHEN THE seat of the Federal Government moved from New York to Philadelphia, Vice-President John Adams was forced to give up his lease on the famous Mortier Mansion at Richmond Hill. For years Aaron Burr had coveted the lovely house, with its wide porticoes, spacious grounds and superb view of the Hudson River and the New Jersey shore. He took over the lease and began to redecorate his prize with a prodigal hand.

He improved the grounds, widened the extensive flower gardens, and dammed a brook to form an attractive pond. For the mansion itself he purchased all manner of furnishings: satin-covered sofas, mahogany armchairs, oriental carpets, elegant mirrors and elaborate crystal chandeliers. The library shelves soon were lined with a shipment of leather-bound books from Burr's London bookseller; the shipment contained works of history, poetry, economics and philosophy, including volumes of Gibbon, William Godwin and Jeremy Bentham.

No expense was spared—and new debts were added to older ones. Burr borrowed from friends, business associates, usurers, paying interest rates of 10, 12, and even 15 percent. But he really didn't care. At some future date he would manage to settle his debts. Meanwhile, he and his wife and child were established in the most elegant summer house in the city where they could live in a gracious style befitting a recently elected Senator and his family.

While Burr was serving in the Senate, Theodosia's long illness mercifully drew to an end. For months she had been bedridden and forced to take daily doses of laudanum to deaden her pain. Burr knew she did not have long to live and wished to leave his Senate duties in Philadelphia to return to her side. But Theodosia insisted that he remain in the capital. When she died at Richmond Hill on May 18, 1794, only her young daughter, Theodosia, was with her.

The death of his wife had a profound and danger-ous effect on Burr. For a dozen years she had been the most stabilizing element in his life. Through the power of her love she had exerted a strong moral in-fluence on a man who was all too prone to hasty and unprincipled conduct, and now that moral influence was gone.

During their marriage, Burr apparently had been a faithful husband, but after his wife's death he threw aside restraint and began to indulge in an endless suc-cession of amorous adventures, so that before long he had gained a notorious reputation. His spending became even more reckless, while his plans to grasp political power grew more bold and enterprising. His swelling ambition, once muted and concealed, now began to emerge and express itself. At last the day came when the name of Colonel Aaron Burr rarely was linked with his past military exploits and deeds of patriotism, but rather with his current practice of political manipulation and chicanery.

Following the death of his wife, Burr undoubtedly was an unhappy man. Proud and aloof, he had many acquaintances, but hardly any true friends. In his loneliness his surviving daughter Theodosia became increasingly the center of his life. She was then a girl of eleven, a lovely, dark-haired child of extraordinary intelligence, vivacity and charm.

Burr long ago had devised an original and ambitious program to educate his talented child. At heart he was as enthusiastic a teacher as his father, the Reverend Aaron Burr, or his grandfather, the illustrious Jonathan Edwards. But he outstripped both in the novelty of his ideas.

In an age that did not think women the possessors of high intelligence, he insisted that girls should receive as much schooling as boys. If the women one met in polite society were silly, empty-headed creatures, he said, it wasn't their fault, it was the fault of their parents who had failed to give them an education. Most had scarcely been taught anything beyond the mere ability to read and write. No wonder they had no grasp of intellectual ideas; no wonder they could not hold a stimulating conversation with an intelligent man.

Burr was determined that Theodosia should have a

superior education. If his idol, Lord Chesterfield, could attempt to form his son into a paragon, why should not Burr himself attempt as much for his beloved Theodosia?

Burr succeeded where Lord Chesterfield had not. The English nobleman was a cold, undemonstrative man; Burr truly loved his daughter, and she knew it. Theodosia responded by adoring—perhaps excessively —her remarkable, strong-willed father. She tried hard to please him. By the age of eleven she could read Greek and Latin and converse fluently in French. She read Gibbon's newly published *Decline and Fall of the Roman Empire*—and may even have enjoyed parts of it. Certainly she enjoyed her music lessons and her lessons with her dancing master. She was a capable horsewoman in an age when few women rode, and an ice skater with more enthusiasm than skill.

She had been a delightful child, and in her early teens became a remarkably poised and mature young woman. She possessed an astonishing amount of social ease, and after her mother's death was accustomed to serve as her father's hostess at Richmond Hill. There she entertained men as urbane as Talleyrand and Volney and other French ex-patriates who had been driven across the seas by the French Revolution.

But she must have been excessively worldly and cynical, too. Her father was a disciple of Chesterfield, and some of his letters showed the English nobleman's unfortunate influence. How to get on in the world— that was always the question. Before she was twelve, Theodosia received lessons in wordliness as well as in Gibbon.

"In case you should dine with Mrs.——" Burr once wrote to her, "I will apprize you of one circumstance, by a trifling attention to which you may elevate yourself in her esteem. She is a great advocate for a very plain, rather abstemious diet in children. . . . Be careful, therefore, to eat but of one dish; that a plain roast or boiled; little or no gravy or butter, and *very sparingly* of dessert or fruit; not more than a half glass of wine; and if more of anything to eat or drink is offered, decline it. If they ask any reason—*Papa thinks it not good for me,* is the best that can be given." And that was how Theodosia, through a touch of hypocrisy, pleased and flattered one of her hostesses.

Burr's term in the Senate brought him to national prominence and made him a figure of recognized political importance. By 1794, with Washington and Adams serving their second term, the anti-Federalists had become a cohesive party. Now they called themselves Republicans. In opposition to the Federalists, they supported France rather than England abroad, and agricultural interests rather than banking and manufacturing interests at home. They were still the minority party, but their numbers and strength were growing. Burr was an effective leader in the Senate and often served as his party's spokesman there.

Apparently the way to even greater power was now open to him. But there were complex and hidden snares on every side. Thomas Jefferson was the party leader. He and his chief disciple, James Madison, had met Clinton and Burr in New York as early as 1791 and made an alliance with them. Jefferson and Madison knew they could manage Clinton and his forces since Clinton had few national ambitions. By 1794, however, it was clear that handling Burr and preventing him from taking control of the Republican Party could turn out to be a more difficult matter.

Oliver Wolcott, Alexander Hamilton's successor as Secretary of the Treasury, described what a Virginia politician said of Burr at this time.

> The two most efficient actors on the political theater of our country are Mr. Hamilton and Mr. Burr. . . . I have watched the movements of Mr. Burr with attention, and have discovered traits of character which sooner or later will give us [the Republicans] much trouble. He has an unequalled talent of attaching men to his views, and forming combinations of which he is always the center. He is determined to play a first part; he acts strenuously with us in public, but it is remarkable that in all private conversation he more frequently agrees with us in principle than in the mode of giving them effect. . . . I shall not be surprised if Mr. Burr is found, in a few years, the leader of a popular party in the northern states; and if this event ever happens, this party will subvert the influence of the southern states.

Here, then, was the key to future developments. Jefferson and the Virginians already were growing fearful of Burr. He offered a threat to their supremacy and to the interest of the landed aristocracy of Virginia. Burr menaced Virginia's leadership of the Republican Party. Soon they decided to edge this dangerous New Yorker away from the center of political power.

The conflict between Jefferson and Burr, between the Virginia Republicans and one band of Republicans in New York, did not come into the open for a number of years. It remained a kind of secret guerrilla war. Burr, recognizing its existence, should have prepared himself to deal at some future time with opponents within his own party. That he failed to do so is one of the most perplexing aspects of his career.

In the meantime, though, he did begin to build and fortify his own political position. He extended his influence in the Society of St. Tammany, New York's original "Tammany Hall." The society then was a working-class social club, composed mainly of poor mechanics and laborers. Many of the members were not qualified voters, for at the time a man had to possess a certain amount of wealth before he was eligible to cast a ballot. But Burr foresaw that conditions might change eventually; gradually he organized the members into a docile army that one day could march to the polls and vote at his bidding—should its members ever obtain the franchise.

He also gathered around him a small band of enthusiastic young men whose fanatic loyalty to himself alone was unquestioned. They included William P. Van Ness, Matthew L. Davis, John, Robert, and Samuel Swartwout, Theodorus Bailey, and Burr's stepson John Prevost. These were Burr's "Myrmidons," as Hamilton called them sneeringly, or Burr's "Tenth Legion," as Theodosia later called them admiringly. They were indeed excellent subordinates. They carried out Burr's commands without hesitation. They were his indispensable lieutenants who marshaled the popular forces in the city for election day battles. Eventually, through his "Myrmidons," Burr was able to form America's first disciplined political machine.

Using Van Ness and the others, Burr worked hard for the Republicans in New York City during the election of 1796. When the national results were tabulated, the Federalists had barely elected John Adams to the Presidency. In the Electoral College he had 71 votes, while Jefferson, the chief Republican, had 68. Jefferson became Vice-President, the first elected by his party. Pinckney, a Federalist, had 59 votes in the College, and in fourth place came Aaron Burr, with 30.

Burr should have received more votes. He had given his full support to Jefferson, but the Virginian had withheld support from him. The Virginia delegates gave Burr only one vote; Jefferson had instructed them to scatter their votes among several favorite sons and to ignore the New Yorker.

Burr realized that he had been dealt with shabbily, but he kept his temper and showed no ill will in public. His position was a difficult one. He had committed himself to the Republicans and had no choice but to go along with them, even though the leader of the party had proved that between Virginia and New York there could never be complete trust and a full accord.

Patience is sometimes a politician's most effective refuge. Burr continued to build his little band in New York and to extend his influence among the workers in the city. And he continued to watch and wait. His day

was coming, slowly perhaps, but coming nevertheless.
Watch and wait, and then, when the time finally arrived, climb still higher, despite Jefferson in his own
party, despite Hamilton and the Federalists in open
opposition. Burr knew himself to be alone in the game
—and alone, somehow, he would triumph.

18.

The Election of 1800

ALMOST TWENTY YEARS now had elapsed since Burr's retirement from the army. During all that time his debts never had ceased to grow. At last his creditors began to lose patience; they pressed him more closely, demanded higher interest, or insisted on a speedy liquidation of their loans.

Burr scurried about frantically, in a debtor's maze, seeking a way out. Again and again he was forced to ask his creditors for a new delay. "When I took your last endorsement payable at *twenty* days," he wrote on one occasion, "I expected that the sale of my property would have been completed before the expiration of that time. It has happened otherwise and the note becomes payable today which obliges me to ask for a further endorsement."

By 1796 he was in grave financial straits. "As to pecuniary matters," he told a friend who had loaned him money, "I am very sorry both for your sake and my own that I can say nothing agreeable. I have met with the most vexatious and ruinous disappointments, and it is, I assure you, with extreme difficulty that I keep along."

Towards the end of the year the entire edifice of notes, loans, and endorsements was tottering. To make matters worse, his distress had become the object of common gossip. His former army friend Robert Troup, now a political opponent, wrote to Rufus King, the American Minister to Great Britian, describing Burr's plight. According to Troup, Burr "during the present session paid little or no attention to his duties in the Senate. It is whispered that his money engagements are embarrassing to him."

And so they were. General John Lamb was one of the principal victims of Burr's financial excesses. On December 9, 1796, Burr wrote to him, asking for "the other 2000 before three o'clock." The next day Burr wrote again, this time saying, "it is with reluctance that I ask your endorsement to the enclosed." On the 17th he sent Lamb additional notes to be renewed. But the general was having his difficulties, too, and could do no more.

There was no escaping the inevitable; Burr had to retrench. He put up for sale some of his dearest personal possessions, and on June 17, 1797, Sir John Temple, the British Consul General, bought "all . . . the household goods, furniture, and things mentioned and expressed in the inventory . . . hereto annexed, and now remaining in the Mansion house and on the farm and piece of land belonging to the said Aaron Burr."

The princely dream which had been Richmond Hill was gone, the elegant, gracious, aristocratic life no longer could be maintained. The elaborate crystal chandeliers, the Turkish carpets, the mahogany armchairs, even the library of leather-bound books, were sold for a fraction of their original cost.

But this was merely the beginning. Burr still was not free of the clamorous creditors who besieged him; indeed, he never was to be free of them again. In 1798 he wrote to General Lamb from Albany asking for further assistance. His personal property was about to be seized—could Lamb come to his aid? The general did, and, for his pains, was arrested himself in 1799. Burr obtained his release, and Lamb, probably with a shudder of relief, disappeared from the scene, never to play a part again in the long chronicle of Burr's financial woes.

Other men, however, soon took the general's place —new friends, relatives, strangers—and found themselves entangled in a similar round of endorsements to be extended, payments to be met, notes to be discounted and exchanged. And always, for Burr, there loomed the specter of complete ruin, public disgrace, and confinement in the cell of a debtor's prison.

Such was the desperate state of Burr's financial affairs as his senatorial term came to a close. Politically, his situation was equally grim. Within the Republican Party he was mistrusted by many prominent leaders. Jefferson and the rest of the Virginians, anxious to control the party, promised to remain a permanent roadblock in his path. Nor could Burr—whatever his inclinations—change allegiance and join the

Federalists as long as Hamilton was at their head. For Hamilton hated and feared him as much as Jefferson did.

In 1797, Burr knew that he had no chance to win another term in the Senate. The New York Legislature was controlled by the Federalists, who were bound to select one of their own number as the new Senator. No other important position was open to him. Seemingly he was at a dead end.

Burr realized that if he were to rise again, he first had to humble himself. Without hesitation he did so. A recognized figure in the national party, a leading Senator for six years, a man who had received thirty votes in the Electoral College only the year before, he swallowed his pride and ran for the lowly position of Assemblyman from the City of New York. He won that local election. And then, from the obscurity of the New York State Assembly, he began the long climb back to national prominence and power.

During the next four years, Burr worked tirelessly to restore his political fortunes and those of the Republican Party in New York State. He overlooked no opportunity, he missed no trick. Dexterously, patiently, with the intuitive cunning of the successful professional politician, he examined every contour of the battlefield, measured the strength of every man and company, and planned every move necessary to defeat the enemy.

He had innumerable obstacles to overcome. One was the advantage enjoyed by the Federalists, who controlled the only two banks in the state. A bank,

Burr knew, was an indispensable political weapon. It could loan money to influential citizens and bind them and their allies to either party; it could pour out funds before a critical election and often change the result. But the state legislature, where the Federalists had a safe majority, would never authorize the incorporation of a Republican bank. Burr saw that somehow he would have to hoodwink his opponents into authorizing such a bank, without allowing them to know what they were doing.

One day he introduced a bill into the New York Assembly authorizing the formation of a water company to supply pure drinking water to New York City within ten years' time. Hidden in the bill was an additional authorization permitting the water company to loan money and carry out other financial transactions with whatever surplus funds it might have available.

With Burr to guide it through the legislature, the apparently harmless bill was passed by the unsuspecting Federalists. The Manhattan Company was incorporated—but no wooden pipes were ever laid, no dams or conduits built, no pure drinking water delivered to the thirsty citizens of the city. Instead, the company began to function as Burr had intended—as a bank, controlled by the Republicans for their own purposes. Later, when the Federalists cried "Fraud" and "Foul," their protests came too late to do them any good.

Though busy with party affairs in the Assembly, Burr did not neglect New York City where his principal strength was concentrated. In time he gained absolute control of the Society of St. Tammany, and completed its conversion from an innocuous social club into an efficient and obedient part of his private political army. His chief lieutenants, Matthew L. Davis, William P. Van Ness, the Swartwout brothers, and numbers more, became officers of the society. At their command, the rank-and-file members could be counted on to vote unfailingly for any candidate who had been selected by their invisible chief, Colonel Aaron Burr.

Yet the Society of St. Tammany was not as useful an instrument as it might have been. Voting requirements had been little changed by 1800; a citizen still had to own a certain amount of land or other property to qualify as an eligible voter, and many of the society's members owned no land or property at all. Burr solved the problem by discovering a legal technicality that would circumvent the law—a practice at which he was singularly adept. He had the members, sometimes as many as thirty or forty, purchase property as joint tenants; the trick was that under the law, each participant in such a purchase then was considered an "owner" of the entire property and automatically became a qualified voter. To make it possible for the members of St. Tammany to buy property, money was loaned to them by the Manhattan Company—an extra dividend from Burr's water company scheme which had an important effect on the Presidential election of 1800.

As that critical election drew nearer, Burr worked with redoubled energy. He was urged on by private letters from Jefferson, in Virginia, the Republican

Party's acknowledged choice for President. Jefferson knew that his own success depended on Burr's ability to carry New York State for the party, so he encouraged Burr and used Burr's efforts to gain power for himself. By doing so, he incurred a political debt to the New Yorker which he had no intention of repaying if he could avoid it.

Burr's activities prior to the election were a model of thoroughness and efficiency. By then he had composed a dossier on every eligible voter in the city. He knew each man's past and present political opinions, his habits, vices, personality, health, and how difficult or easy it was to get him to the polls.

Some of Burr's agents solicited funds for the party by a house-to-house canvas; others used a special list of wealthy voters, drawn up for the express purpose of siphoning money into the party's war chest.

Burr decreed that each wealthy citizen on the list had to be treated individually. The man's psychology was all-important. Burr's lieutenants, for example, had marked down one citizen for a contribution of $100. The man was notably stingy, however, and Burr was sure he would not contribute a penny. "Strike out his name," Burr told them. "You will not get the money, his exertions on our behalf will cease, and you will not even see him at the polls." Another man was remarkably lazy. Burr realized he would contribute money, but do no work. "Double the amount of his contribution," Burr said, "and tell him no labor will be expected of him."

There was even more to be done. Burr arranged meetings and rallies in every precinct and ward, provided a steady supply of effective and well-informed speakers, and made a number of speeches himself in an attempt to persuade the uncommitted to cast a Republican ballot and to hold the regular Republican forces steady in the face of enemy blandishments and threats. Despite all these efforts, the Federalists were still the stronger party prior to the election, and the Presidency should have been theirs once again. But then, during the last days of the campaign, the Federalist leader, Alexander Hamilton, made a grave blunder.

Actually, the Federalists were a party in decline, torn by factional dissension and personal jealousies. Hamilton and President John Adams detested one another. Hamilton hoped to gain the Presidency in 1800 for another Federalist, Charles Pinckney, of South Carolina. To undermine Adams, and to promote Pinckney's cause, Hamilton wrote a secret pamphlet highly critical of Adams to which he unwisely signed his name.

Only a few copies of the inflammable pamphlet were printed, and these were placed exclusively in the hands of "trustworthy" Federalists. But the ink was hardly dry when Burr's "intelligence service got wind of what Hamilton had done. Within a few hours Burr had a copy of the pamphlet. The next day the Republican newspapers printed it. The disclosure split the Federalist forces into warring camps and allowed the Republicans to slip between them and carry the election.

The vote of New York State proved decisive. A switch of a mere 250 votes in New York City would have handed the entire state to the Federalists. Instead, New York went to the Republicans, and with it, the Presidency. The victory had been engineered by Aaron Burr; it was a fact recognized throughout the nation.

Yet the election of 1800 was far from over. A count in the Electoral College revealed an unprecedented situation: Jefferson and Burr, with 73 votes apiece, were tied for the Presidency.

The Republican delegates in the Electoral College had *meant*, of course, to vote first for Jefferson and second for Burr—in other words, to elect Jefferson President and Burr Vice-President. But because of a defect in the Constitution, they had no means of indicating their intention, no way of showing that their "presidential" votes had been meant for Jefferson, their "vice-presidential" votes meant for Burr. The two votes cast by a delegate were indistinguishable from each other, and so now the ballots had been cast and counted and there was a tie, 73–73. The issue between Jefferson and Burr would have to be decided by a new vote, this time in the House of Representatives, where the Federalists still had considerable strength and were determined to accomplish as much mischief as possible.

While the members of the House were gathering in Washington to elect a President, Burr was in Albany attending the wedding of his daughter to Joseph Alston, a wealthy young planter from South Carolina.

Burr was foolish to absent himself from the capital during the week of the critical election in the House. He should have remained in Washington, quieting Jefferson's fears and reassuring the Virginian that he was not trying to steal the Presidency.

It is easy to understand why such rumors were being heard in the capital. Because of the unexpected tie in the Electoral College, the Federalists were able to influence the choice between Jefferson and Burr. Most Federalists preferred Burr for President. The New Yorker's republicanism was not as uncompromising as Jefferson's. With Burr as President, the Federalists reasoned, there would always be the chance for an accommodation. With Jefferson as President, there could only be enmity and war. So the Federalists tried to form an alliance with Burr, and though he refused to listen to their offers, the rumors of a "deal" persisted and spread.

Almost alone among the Federalists, Hamilton stood against Burr. Despite the fact that he and Jefferson had been bitter political antagonists for nearly a decade, he urged the Federalist members of the House to vote for Jefferson. Had he not, Burr would have carried the vote on the first ballot. Hamilton's activities were not lost on Burr. He filed the memory away; it was merely one of a number of grievances he held against Hamilton. Should the occasion arise, he would be happy to repay it in full.

The first roll call was taken in the House of Representatives on February 11, 1801. Each state had a single vote; by then, there were sixteen states in the Union, and a majority—at least nine— was required for election.

When the roll call was finished, Jefferson had won eight states, Burr six; two—Maryland and Vermont— were tied. Neither candidate held a majority; the House was deadlocked, and no one could say when the issue would be settled.

In all, it took thirty-six roll calls and almost a week of incessant behind-the-scenes activity before a single Representative could be induced to change his vote. During that time, the switch of one man in any of six delegations would have given the election to Jefferson. The switch of only three delegates would have given the election to Burr. As to an absolute majority, Burr held the lead, 55 to 51. On that basis he would have been chosen on the first ballot.

At last, on February 17th, several Representatives did switch their votes. In the final tabulation, Jefferson had ten states, Burr four, with two states casting a blank ballot. Thomas Jefferson thus became the third President of the United States, and Aaron Burr became his Vice-President.

The most curious aspect of the special election was the way Burr conducted himself. Despite the unfounded claims of his enemies, there is no evidence that he sought to gain the Presidency and there is considerable evidence that he spurned every offer of a deal.

There is the testimony of Federalist James A. Bayard, the sole Representative from the state of

Delaware. After the election Bayard wrote to Hamilton:

The means existed of electing Burr, but this required his cooperation. By deceiving one man (a great blockhead), and tempting two (not incorruptible), he might have secured a majority of the States. He will never have another chance of being President of the United States; and the little use he has made of the one which has occurred, gives me but an humble opinion of [his] talents. . . .

A letter written by a Federalist Representative during some of the innumerable roll calls said:

We have postponed until tomorrow 11 o'clock, the voting for president. All stand firm. Jefferson eight—Burr six—divided two. Had Burr done anything for himself, he would long ere this have been president. If a majority would answer, he would have had it on every vote.

If these accounts are to be believed, Aaron Burr, a man long avid for political power, unaccountably turned his back on the highest office in the land at the very moment when that office was his. But is that what Burr really did? *Could* he have become the President of the United States in 1801, or was the possibility little more than an illusion?

It is likely that Burr saw through the tangle of events, and decided that the Presidency was not truly within his grasp. The majority of Americans wanted Jefferson for President, not him. If he were to make a deal with the discredited Federalists, there would be cries of "Fraud!"—justifiable cries—and he would be called a usurper, not a President.

Burr may have realized that the popular will in America could not be flaunted with impunity. There would be uprisings, possibly a general revolt. Worse still, Virginia would secede; Jefferson and his cohorts already had threatened to lead their state out of the Union if Jefferson were deprived of office by a legalistic swindle. Who could say how many other states might follow Virginia? And then what would Burr be President of —a nation in arms, a nation divided into three of four confederacies? He might be president of one, but he would hardly be President of the United States.

Instead, why not resist the temptation to seize an unlawful prize? By rebuffing the Federalists now he might guarantee the Presidency for himself in a few years' time through legitimate succession. He was already Vice-President. He and Jefferson would run again in four years; with the Federalists a shattered party, their ticket was bound to win. Then, after his second term in office, Jefferson would follow Washington's example and retire to private life. Aaron Burr, the Vice-President, would then receive his party's nomination, and in 1808 the Presidency would be his.

Such probably was the reasoning of Burr as he rejected the Federalists in 1801 and refused their illusory offer of the Presidency. No one can say for certain, however, because he did not commit his calculations to paper or confide them to friends. The plan was a reasonable one, but it contained a dangerous assumption: that Jefferson, who had proved untrustworthy in 1796, could be counted on to repay his political debts in the future. How Jefferson did repay them, Aaron Burr was to learn—and far more quickly than he could have imagined.

19.

Gratitude and Revenge

B URR'S CAREER had now reached its zenith. As
Vice-President he held the second highest elective
office in the country. He had built an irresistible political army in New York City and had used it to win
the election of 1800 for the Republican Party. His
rise had been fantastically swift. From the obscurity of
the New York Assembly he had reached a position of
national preeminence against great odds in less than a
half-dozen years.

The very swiftness of his success, however, produced
unfortunate consequences. It increased the fears of his
political adversaries. It aroused the jealousy of former
friends. And it did something even more insidious—it
strengthened Burr's belief in his own infallibility.
Hadn't he accomplished a miracle in 1800? Then why
should he not continue to produce an endless string of
miracles, to sweep aside all opposition, to add triumph
to triumph? Thus, when Burr's judgment should have

been keenest, it was thoroughly dulled by pride and self-delusion. At the very moment when hidden enemies were beginning to plot his destruction, he believed himself to be indestructible.

The main effort to ruin Burr was not engineered by Alexander Hamilton, his avowed political rival, but by Thomas Jefferson, his recent ally and the head of the victorious party to which they both belonged. Jefferson acted as he did from a variety of motives. He could not forget his debt to Burr, and the remembrance of it was a constant source of humiliation. Instead of feeling gratitude toward Burr, who had elevated him to the Presidency, Jefferson, a proud man, felt an intolerable resentment.

Added to this was the Virginian's genuine and well-founded mistrust of the New Yorker. Jefferson had suspected for years that Burr was a thorough opportunist. He believed Burr's republicanism was only skin-deep—as indeed it was—and that the Vice-President adhered to party principles more as a matter of political expedience than from any deep-rooted personal conviction. The rise of such a man to eminence and power in the national government was a cause of genuine distress to President Jefferson.

These really were lesser issues, though. The main issue was the fact that only a single man threatened the supremacy of Jefferson and his Virginians within the Republican Party. That man was the Vice-President. Burr had to be stripped of all power, broken, and, if necessary, driven out of the party itself.

The destruction of Burr could not be accomplished by a single stroke. It required time, careful planning, and secrecy. And so, step by step, Jefferson began to carry out his design, working clandestinely, so that for as long as possible Burr would neither perceive nor understand the maneuvers against him.

First, to undermine Burr's position in his own state, Jefferson cut him off from his former political allies: the Livingstons, who now led one Republican faction in New York; and old Governor Clinton and his young nephew, De Witt Clinton, who led another. Jefferson enticed the Livingstons away from Burr by offering them the high government positions they long had sought. The leader of the Livingston clan became the new Minister to France. Another member became Mayor of New York at $10,000 a year, as well as the Attorney General. A third became Secretary of State, a fourth a United States Senator. Several other family members were rewarded with various judgeships in New York.

Then, to gain the adherence of the Clintons, Jefferson offered them the politician's ultimate weapon: the power of patronage. There were many Federal jobs in New York that had to be filled. Jefferson made the appointments in Washington, but only after consultation with the Clintons in New York. As a result, the friends and supporters of the Clintons got most of the Federal jobs in the state while the friends and supporters of Burr received few or none. A politician who cannot reward his followers with good jobs is a politician in decline. That was what Aaron Burr had become.

By now it should have been obvious to Burr that something was seriously amiss. The atmosphere toward him in official Washington was chilly; he took no part in the work of the administration, he wielded little power, his opinions were rarely sought. Worse still, the President, though always polite, nevertheless delayed each time Burr renewed his request that he be given a few political jobs for his supporters in New York.

But Burr, blinded by pride and overconfidence, still did not see exactly what was happening. He still did not recognize that the Livingstons had deserted him and that De Witt Clinton was a terribly ambitious young man who wished to crush him.

There were other political jobs in New York that were filled by local rather than by Presidential appointment. Burr could have kept such appointments to himself and retained his strength within the state. But he failed to do so. He let the power of appointment fall into the hands of his enemies. As a result, the Clintons filled job after job with their own henchmen. Burr's followers again received nothing. Soon the ranks of Burr's army began to dwindle. The ranks of the Clintonites began to swell.

With no patronage left in his control, with no ability to reward his followers, with the state machinery in the hands of the Clintons, and with the Livingstons fled to the side of his enemies, Burr's political power was almost crushed, and Jefferson's design almost completed. The congressional elections of 1802 only contributed to Burr's destruction. Republicans everywhere were triumphant. The Federalists were now a party in permanent decline. Looking ahead to 1804, it was easy to see that Jefferson would be reelected by a landslide and that whatever strength Burr still retained in New York would not be needed by the party. From that time on, the atmosphere in official Washington grew even chillier toward the Vice-President.

To all practical effects, Burr now had been successfully driven out of the Republican Party. He had no hope of retaining the Vice-Presidency in 1804, or of succeeding Jefferson to the Presidency in 1808. His political dreams were smashed, his future empty. Encumbered by massive private debts, his public career in ruins, Burr truly was a desperate man. Such men often turn to desperate measures—and Aaron Burr proved no exception.

During the spring of 1803, the United States bought the huge western territory of Louisiana from Napoleon Bonaparte, the ruler of France. Overwhelmingly approved by the people of America, the Louisiana Purchase signaled the final destruction of the Federalist Party. The strength of the Federalists always had been centered in the eastern section of the country. Its most fervent supporters had been members of the banking and merchant classes along the Atlantic Coast. The West was solidly Republican. With the purchase of the Louisiana Territory, more and more western states eventually would join the Union, leaving the Federalist Party even more feeble than it had become by 1803.

Realizing this, a small group of die-hard New England Federalists formed a plan to lead their states out of the Union and create an independent northern confederation where Federalism would continue to

flourish. The principal leaders of this secessionist conspiracy were Congressman Griswold of Connecticut
and four disaffected New England Senators: Picker-
ing, Plumer, Tracy, and Hillhouse. They soon realized,
however, that the proposed confederation had no
chance of success unless wealthy and populous New
York State became a part of it. To bring this about,
they had to capture the governorship of New York. It
was not long before they began to think of Aaron
Burr.

The New England conspirators approached him,
explained their plans, and offered him Federalist support in New York State if he would run for Governor.
A bargain was made, though Burr was far too wily to
acknowledge the offer publicly or to state the terms of
the agreement.

The offer of Federalist support fitted in well with
Burr's own plans. In 1804 he would run for Governor
of New York as an Independent Republican. His opponent would be Morgan Lewis, the official Republican Party candidate, who had the support of the Livingstons and the Clintons.

Burr had two hopes of success. Should he become
Governor, and should his Federalist partners win the
New England states, he could then lead New York into
the new confederation and become its President. But
if he should win, while his Federalist partners failed,
he would be almost equally well off. As Governor of
New York he would regain the power of patronage in
the state which he had so foolishly allowed to slip from
his grasp. Then he would have his day of revenge. The
Livingstons and the Clintons would be swept from

office; their henchmen would be deprived of all the choice political plums they had been feeding on, and his own supporters would begin to feed on those choice plums instead.

It was then that Alexander Hamilton roused himself from political retirement and began to battle with his old-time fury to block Burr's upward march. Hamilton wrote dozens of pamphlets, conferred endlessly with Federalist Party leaders, and urged them with all the persuasion at his command to turn away from Burr and the secessionist plot. It was bitter medicine for Hamilton that his own party should support a scheme to destroy the Union for which he had labored so hard and back his own worst political enemy in promoting that scheme.

But Election Day, 1804, provided even more bitter medicine for Burr. Hamilton's opposition had been enough, and Morgan Lewis was elected Governor.

The rest of the election news was equally grim for Burr. The Federalists had lost all of New England except Connecticut and had managed to carry only one other state in the Union, tiny Delaware. The secessionist conspiracy was dead, and could not be revived. Nor could Burr's own political hopes. He had nowhere to turn. He had deserted the Republican ranks and had failed the Federalists. He was—politically as well as financially—an utter bankrupt.

Deprived of his revenge against the Livingstons and Clintons and of a chance to rebuild his political fortunes in New York, Burr decided to revenge himself on his old antagonist, Alexander Hamilton. During the campaign for Governor, certain remarks insulting to Burr had appeared in an Albany newspaper. The remarks were attributed to Hamilton. Burr waited until two months after their appearance, and then wrote to Hamilton asking for an explanation.

Hamilton's reply neither affirmed nor denied that the remarks had been his. Burr wrote again, stating that his honor as a gentleman required "satisfaction" for the insult and that he would meet Hamilton in a duel at a time and place to be arranged.

Burr's immediate object was to kill Hamilton. He long had hated the great Federalist who had attempted to thwart his rise to power for a dozen years. Perhaps, too, Burr believed that with Hamilton dead, his own political future would brighten. Exactly how he expected this to come about, however, it is impossible to say.

Burr, of course, did not record his thoughts at the time he issued the challenge to Hamilton, nor did he do so later. No one can be sure what all of his motives might have been. Yet one thing is certain: by 1804 Burr had become a dissolute and desperate adventurer. His moral defects no longer could be hidden; he was ready for any enterprise—war, secession, treason, murder—as long as it did not violate his singular "code of honor" and fitted his private schemes.

The challenge was accepted by Hamilton. At seven o'clock on the morning of July 11, 1804, the two men met on a notorious dueling ground at Weehawken, New Jersey, across the Hudson River from New York. Unlike Burr, Hamilton had no thought of hitting his rival. His intention was to fire his own shot harmlessly and to hope that Burr would miss. He wished only to escape the stigma of cowardice. For this reason alone he had agreed to the duel.

Burr did not miss, however. He shot Hamilton in the side, just under the heart. Hamilton rose on his toes, and spun around, his pistol discharging above his head. Then he fell. The physician attending the duel examined him and said he was gravely wounded.

Hamilton was brought back to New York where he lay in great pain for thirty-one hours before he died. At the news of his death, there was a tremendous public outcry against Burr. Partly this was the work of the Clintonites, who wished to be certain that their political archrival would be so completely disgraced that he never again could challenge them. Partly, though, it was the natural response of the people of New York, who knew both men well by their past words and actions. They felt that Burr, disappointed in the recent gubernatorial election, had callously sought out a rival and murdered him for political expediency and personal revenge.

Burr was mystified by the storm that arose against him. He never had anticipated such a furor of rage and disgust. Other gentlemen fought duels, and sometimes killed their rivals, yet no storm arose against *them*. Why should he alone be singled out for infamy? The situation was one for which the *Letters* of Lord Chesterfield, despite their cynical wisdom, had left Burr unprepared.

He remained in New York for eleven days, vainly hoping the storm would subside. A coroner's jury held an inquiry into the duel and proposed that Burr be indicted for murder.

On July 21st he slipped away from his home and fled to Perth Amboy, New Jersey. Then he went to Philadelphia. By that time indictments had been issued against him in both New York and New Jersey. Though the charges eventually were dropped, they made him for a time a fugitive from justice.

Incredibly enough, Burr was not downhearted. It was true that he had lost a number of battles, but he still hadn't lost the war. He already had new plans afoot; indeed, he had been forming them for several years, watching events, waiting for the moment to strike. That moment was drawing nearer.

To the south and west there were vast, empty territories, some of them a part of the United States, some still colonies owned by Spain. It was a region where a bold man like himself at the head of a small band of loyal followers could achieve great things.

With eight months of his term as Vice-President still remaining, Aaron Burr, a fugitive from a charge of murder, departed for the South. His character, which had begun to weaken after the death of his wife, was now completely corrupted. He was a cold-blooded opportunist, ready to seize any advantage that presented itself, no matter how despicable that advantage might be.

20.

The Conspirator

BURR'S TRIP south in 1804 took him to East Florida, at that time a colony of Spain, where he journeyed through the countryside, drawing maps and gathering any information which might prove useful in the future. Turning north, he visited his son-in-law, Joseph Alston, his daughter, Theodosia, and his beloved grandson, Aaron Burr Alston, whom he called "Gamp," at their home in Charleston, South Carolina. Finally he returned to the capital in Washington.

By that time the murder charge against him had been dropped and some of the furor over his killing of Hamilton had grown less strident. In much of the East, however, he still was a social outcast, and in Washington he was excluded from the homes of everyone of importance. In Washington he learned that during his travels in the South his New York house had been sold for $25,000 to satisfy some of his creditors. He still owed at least $8,000 more that he was unable to repay. Except for his salary, and whatever money he could raise by fresh borrowing, he was penniless.

Burr still had several months to serve as Vice-President. While in Washington he began to scheme in earnest. He formulated plans; he spun the first strands of complicated plots; he talked with friends and hinted that the time might soon be ripe for them to band together in an exciting enterprise which would bring them great wealth and glory. Burr, in fact, had found a new career. He had become a professional conspirator.

As the weeks passed in Washington, his thoughts turned increasingly to the West. As early as 1802 he had sensed that in the huge and largely unsettled region beyond the Allegheny Mountains there was room for a man like himself to become rich and powerful.

The opportunities were many and varied, the circumstances complex and subject to constant change. One possibility lay in the new states of Kentucky, Tennessee and Ohio, and in the rest of the Northwest Territory. Here was a region where the settlers were traditionally independent, where feelings of loyalty to the eastern United States and the government in Washington were not always fervent. Here the idea of Separatism—the forming of a separate and independent country—had often been advocated.

Another possibility lay further south and west. Here was a much larger region, some of it partially settled by Americans, much of it empty or inhabited only by Indians. The area included the Mississippi Territory, between the Tennessee and Mississippi rivers, and the Louisiana and Orleans territories, to the west of the Mississippi. It would be a splendid place for land speculators to operate, to buy up millions of acres for almost nothing, and then resell them to newly arriving settlers from the East for huge profits. It also was an area where an independent country could easily be established by enterprising men.

Finally, beyond the Sabine River to the southwest, was Mexico. A huge colony, weakly held by the local Spanish government, it was a prize to stir the imagination of any adventurer. Add Mexico to the Territories of Louisiana and Orleans and you would have a handsome kingdom. To this add the Mississippi Territory, the Northwest Territory, the states of Kentucky, Tennessee and Ohio, and you would have a vast and rich empire worthy of the governing talents of Bonaparte himself. These were some of the feverish dreams of Aaron Burr, the Vice-President of the United States.

Burr's principal partner in these treasonous plans now arrived in Washington. He was General James Wilkinson, Burr's old comrade-in-arms. The two had remained friends since their days together in Canada under Benedict Arnold.

Wilkinson's career, from the time of the Revolutionary War, had been filled with intrigue, corruption and dishonor. In 1784 he had moved to Kentucky where he became a merchant, a land speculator, and a politician. In 1787 he went south to New Orleans and met the Spanish Governor. That year Wilkinson became a paid agent of Spain with an annual fee of $2,000, and a traitor to the United States.

Though still in the pay of Spain, Wilkinson rejoined the army and in 1792 was promoted to the rank of brigadier general. In 1794 he fought under General Anthony Wayne against the northern Indians in the Battle of Fallen Timbers. In 1797, though remaining a brigadier, he became the ranking general in the United States. In the same year Spain paid him $16,000 for his traitorous services.

Seven years later, when Wilkinson arrived in Washington to confer with Burr, he had risen even higher. He was the newly appointed Governor of the Territory of Louisiana, the commanding general of all American troops on the Mexican border, and the Commander of the United States Army.

Burr and Wilkinson studied maps of the Southwest and made plans. Their principal hope was that before many months had passed, the United States and Spain would be at war. For several years there had been a dispute between the two countries over the boundaries of West Florida. Should war break out, Burr would immediately join Wilkinson in New Orleans. Together they would set out at the head of an army to "liberate" Mexico from Spain.

Meanwhile, Wilkinson would return to his post, and Burr, traveling west along the Ohio River, would see what support he could gather in Ohio, Kentucky and Tennessee for a separatist movement. Their ultimate aim would be to unite that region with Louisiana and as much of Mexico as they could wrest from Spain.

Before he left Washington, Burr approached the British Minister, Anthony Merry, with another scheme. The settlers in Louisiana, Burr said, were eager to gain their independence. They could do so with the help of England. The creation of an independent Louisiana under British protection, Burr maintained, would bring a number of benefits to both Britain and Louisiana. In order to insure the separation of the territory from the United States, Burr said he would need a half million dollars from England and the use of a British naval squadron to blockade the mouth of the Mississippi River. The British Minister liked the scheme and said he would forward it to his government.

For a time, Burr had high hopes that he would obtain British aid. Eventually, however, the death of the British Prime Minister and a subsequent change of administration brought an end to his English plans. But the setback did not discourage him from other treasonous activities.

21.

Western Schemes

O N APRIL 10, 1805, Burr left for the West. Rumors about his activities had been circulating for some time prior to his departure. In March the French Minister in Washington, Louis Turreau, wrote to Talleyrand, "Louisiana thus is going to be the seat of Mr. Burr's new intrigues; he is going there under the aegis of General Wilkinson." This much, at least, was generally known in diplomatic circles. Also known was the interesting fact that Burr had asked for a passport to Mexico, and that his request had been refused by the Spanish Minister.

By the end of April, Burr reached Pittsburgh where he bought a handsome flatboat sixty feet long. The boat contained a dining room, two bedrooms, four apartments with glass windows, and a kitchen complete with fireplace. The boat cost $133, and no doubt was purchased with borrowed funds.

Burr's progress down the Ohio and Mississippi rivers to New Orleans was most enjoyable. His duel

with Hamilton, which had made him a social outcast
in the East, merely enhanced his prestige in the West
where duels often were fought over questions of
"honor." Burr, lately the nation's Vice-President, was
feted at numerous dinners and banquets. Wherever he went he charmed his hosts with his wit,
urbanity, and polished manners.

As for the object of his voyage—it changed almost
from day to day, depending on the character and political outlook of his listeners. Except with trusted con-
fidants, he discussed only Mexico and the possibility of
war with Spain. He did not mention an independent
Louisiana or a treasonous plot to separate any part of
the West from the remainder of the nation.

Nowhere was Burr more cordially received that
summer than on a small, privately owned island on the
Ohio River. There was the home of Harman Blennerhassett, a wealthy, romantic and eccentric Irishman
who had emigrated to the Ohio Valley a number of
years before. Blennerhassett had built a huge house,
imported a large collection of fruit trees, and added an
extensive library to his dwelling. He had spent a good
deal of his fortune on these and other embellishments
of civilization, which were largely unknown throughout the pioneer West.

Harman Blennerhassett was not at home when
Burr's flatboat arrived, but his wife received the ex-
Vice-President and entertained him for several days.
At the time it was a mere diversion for Burr. But the
next winter, when circumstances had changed, he
remembered the house, orchard, library—and the
apparent wealth of the absent owner.

All seemingly went well in the West that summer. Burr met many friends of Wilkinson and discussed possibilities for future action with them. He was in Natchez in June, and spent most of July in New Orleans. There he met the leaders of a local organization called the Mexican Association; their ambition was to conquer Mexico and take over the country for themselves. Before he left the city, Burr and the Association leaders drew up tentative plans for an invasion of Mexico, with Burr cast in the role of commander in chief.

Rumors about Burr's treasonous activities grew more persistent by late summer and early fall. In order to flourish, an intrigue requires secrecy; both Wilkinson and Burr already had approached too many others and had talked too much about their ambitious schemes. Their indiscretions were endangering the success of their enterprise before they had placed a single soldier in the field or taken possession of a single acre of land.

In the late autumn their plans received a great blow. By that time Burr was back in the capital where President Jefferson informed him of a complicated arrangement which had just been concluded with Napoleon and Talleyrand. For a payment of $2,000,-000, Spain was willing to cede the disputed portions of West Florida to the United States. The boundary quarrel was over. There was not going to be a war with Spain after all.

This promised to be ruinous for Burr and Wilkinson. Without a war, their intrigue would become infinitely more dangerous. Patriotic citizens, who might have supported their invasion of Mexico on the supposition that it furthered the interests of the United States, would never support them in a private adventure which clearly would benefit only themselves.

In January, 1806, Burr was trying to enlist new recruits for his schemes. One of those he approached was William Eaton, the leader of an incredible march across the African desert during the American campaign against the Tripoli pirates. At first Burr was cautious; he told Eaton he planned to invade Mexico, but only with the approval of the United States Government.

Eaton, suspecting there was more to it than that, questioned Burr further. Before long Burr admitted that he planned to separate the West from the Union and form an independent nation, with New Orleans as its capital and with himself as chief of state.

Carried away, Burr went on to declare that if he "could gain over the marine corps and secure to his interests the naval commanders Truxton, Preble, Decatur, and others, he would turn congress out of doors, get rid of the president, and declare himself the protector of an energetic government." In short, according to Eaton, Burr even harbored the fantastic notion of fomenting a revolution in the United States and of declaring himself dictator of the country through a military *coup d'état.*

Nothing came of this scheme, of course, and so Burr's thoughts reverted again to Louisiana and Mexico. Early in the spring of 1806 he wrote Harman Blennerhassett, the eccentric Irish settler, and invited him to join in a western adventure. Burr needed money and thought Blennerhassett's remaining funds could be put to good use. He told Blennerhassett that after they conquered Mexico, he himself would become emperor, with Theodosia his successor, while Blennerhassett would be their Mexican prime minister. Blennerhassett, enchanted with visions of wealth and fame, willingly parted with all the money he could raise.

Later in the spring, Burr's feverish hopes were lifted substantially. Another boundary dispute arose, this time between the Spanish and American forces west of the Mississippi. However, by this time a coolness had developed between Burr and Wilkinson. For several months the general had not answered Burr's letters. The truth was that Wilkinson had grown terrified of exposure. He had much to conceal—twenty years of treasonable activity for the Spanish Government, his plotting with Burr, his own designs on Mexico. Wishing that he had never begun to conspire with Burr, he started to look for a way out of his troubles.

Burr knew none of this. Counting on Wilkinson to supply military support when it might be needed, he went ahead with his preparations, and by midsummer they were completed. He intended to travel west and south, eventually as far as Natchez. There he would wait with his expeditionary force of volunteers until his fellow conspirators in Louisiana declared the territory independent of the United States and invited him to assume the presidency. Then he would proceed to New Orleans where he would invent a pretext to invade Mexico and add it to his empire. It was a wild scheme, but it might have succeeded if everything had gone according to plan.

Burr and a small band of followers started west from Philadelphia in August, 1806. They reached the Ohio River, and sailed to Blennerhassett's Island. For the rest of the autumn, Burr, Blennerhassett and several others were kept busy gathering supplies, raising money, and recruiting additional volunteers.

But rumors about Burr's activities were flying faster than ever now. In Washington, President Jefferson heard more and more alarming reports. Burr was on the Ohio, heading west. Burr was on the Mississippi, heading south. Everyone was talking about his expedition. The whole country seemed aware of Burr's intention to separate the western states and territories from the East and to set himself up as the chief executive of an independent nation.

At last Wilkinson decided he could wait no longer. He wrote a number of letters to the President "alerting" him to a dangerous conspiracy. He assured Jefferson that he would take all necessary steps to counter the insurgent forces when they appeared in the territory; he arrested three of Burr's agents in New Orleans and sent them to Washington. Burr was the archtraitor, Wilkinson shrilly informed the President, and as the loyal Commander of the United States Army Wilkinson would apprehend him!

After Wilkinson's betrayal, the grandiose scheme to separate the West and conquer Mexico quickly collapsed. It took several weeks to arrest Burr and return him to Washington for trial on charges of treason.

Burr's trial in Richmond, Virginia, attracted the attention of the entire country. Jefferson was eager to secure a verdict of guilty against his old political foe. But, despite the reasonable presumption that Burr had been guilty of treason, the Government's case was difficult to prove.

Much of the evidence against Burr was deemed inadmissible on just, but extremely narrow, legal grounds. The key to the proceedings then became this: The constitutional definition of treason was the "levying [of] war against the United States or adhering to their enemies," and such treason could only be proved if "an overt act" had been committed. From this it followed that the mere gathering of an expedition like Burr's, with the *intention* of promoting secession, was not treason if the expedition collapsed before an *act* of treason had been committed. Since Burr's expedition had collapsed before the overt act, the jury decided—after a long and wearisome trial—that no treason had been committed and Burr was declared innocent.

With this decision—unpopular as it was—additional charges against Burr and his followers were dropped.

Wilkinson now came under considerable fire, too. His conduct at the trial and his testimony against Burr had left a strong impression on almost everyone but the President that he had been guilty of treasonous activities for a far longer time than Burr. Jefferson protected him, however, and Wilkinson was judged innocent of all wrongdoing by a court-martial board conveniently comprised of his subordinate officers.

Burr, despite his own acquittal, was an utterly ruined man. He was encumbered by greater debts than ever. His law practice was gone, and the hatred and contempt in which he was held made it impossible for him to think of rebuilding it.

Wherever he went, he was vilified as Hamilton's murderer or as a traitor for his western activities. It was not safe for him to walk on the streets. In Baltimore he was hanged in effigy and forced to flee from a vengeful mob. He was cut by almost everyone he knew, except a few of the loyal Myrmidons. He still had his daughter Theodosia and his grandson Gamp. Otherwise, he was alone in the world.

And yet he refused to give up his hopes for the future. He saw one last chance, one final opportunity to recoup his fortunes. Europe, he believed, was the answer. There, in the foreign chancellories of England and France, were men who held vast power in their hands, men of vision who would listen to his grand designs. He would tell them of Mexico—a field for great activity. Of Louisiana, Canada, the western territories—and who could say, with a man like himself at the head of a bold new enterprise, what goals might not yet be achieved?

On June 7, 1808, Aaron Burr set out for Europe. He was fifty-one years old. He had scarcely any money. To anyone but himself the future would have looked so hopeless that further effort would have been impossible. Despite his many moral defects, Burr possessed one virtue to an astonishing degree—unwavering courage in the face of adversity.

22.

The Dreams Are Over

BURR'S EUROPEAN EXILE lasted four years. During much of that time he was utterly impoverished. On several occasions he was reduced to a diet of bread and potatoes; sometimes, during the coldest winter months, he had no fire in his rented room.

Once or twice he received money from the United States, but Theodosia and her husband had suffered financial reverses, too, and could do little to help him. Somehow Burr managed to stay afloat, borrowing from friends, launching new speculations, and even buying gifts for Theodosia and Gamp, which he usually was forced to pawn before the week was out in order to pay for his cheap lodgings or frugal suppers.

Yet his charm, his political reputation, even his notoriety, opened many doors. He spent days with important politicians and statesmen and evenings with titled lords and ladies before returning alone to his wretched garret. He met and became friends with his old literary idols—Jeremy Bentham, the philosopher and economist; William Godwin, the anarchist and educator; William Cobbett, the essayist. It was a strange existence. Apparently carefree and prosperous, Burr actually was torn by anxieties and often was destitute.

Theodosia's letters from home were frequently delayed for many months, but when they finally came they invariably revived his spirits. Her admiration for her father never flagged. While one failure followed another for Burr, Theodosia watched from afar. She admired, encouraged, and almost never admitted despair.

"I witness your extraordinary fortitude," she wrote, "with new wonder at every misfortune. You appear to me so superior, so elevated above all other men, I contemplate you with such a strange mixture of humility, admiration, reverence, love and pride, that very little . . . would be necessary to make me worship you as a superior being; such enthusiasm does your character excite in me. . . . I had rather not live than not to be the daughter of such a man." One may question the soundness of her judgment, but one cannot question the strength of her loyalty and devotion.

Burr's dreams had become more and more concerned with Theodosia and Gamp. For their sakes he wished to return to the Western Hemisphere in triumph. Mexico was still his great object, his obsession. He was still to become the Emperor of Mexico. Theodosia would become the Empress on his death. When Gamp reached his majority he would inherit the throne of the Burrs.

Britain did not welcome his schemes, however. After several months he was arrested, his papers seized, and he was threatened with deportation. The American Minister, appointed by President Jefferson, reported to the British Government that Burr was still designing, scheming, plotting. In time his passport was restored, and he decided it would be wise to leave the country.

He traveled through Sweden, Denmark, Germany, and in February, 1810, arrived in Paris with a scheme for the Emperor Napoleon. He still hoped to "liberate" Mexico and Louisiana, but would need French support. In exchange, he would procure Canada for Napoleon.

The American people, Burr told French officials, were extremely discontented. They would oppose any change of government *at first*—but the right man could bring about a *coup d'état*. Burr, of course, was the right man.

As his hopes declined, his schemes grew even wilder. Secret French Government papers reported him as saying that in America there was "a third party, superior in talent and energy; they deserve something grand and startling, something which, in giving occupation to active spirits, will assure the tranquillity of reasonable men. This party has a recognized head; they ask only to follow and obey him."

The entire claim, of course, was nonsense. There was no such party, and even if there had been, its members would not have followed Burr. The French listened to his proposals and concluded he wished to set up a monarchy in America, with himself as king.

But there was considerably more to it. Burr told the French there were 40,000 American seamen who had been thrown out of work by Jefferson's embargo. With a French loan, Burr would return to the United States, organize the seamen, and overthrow the government in Washington. A declaration of war against France's enemy, England, then would follow, and Napoleon and Burr would fight together against the common foe. The French, needless to say, did not believe Burr's assertions and refused to become involved in his fantastic dreams.

At length even Burr realized that the desperate game was over. His last cards had been played. England and France, far from being interested in his plans, wished only to be rid of him. Penniless, he pawned his overcoat to help pay for his passage home.

Four years had elapsed since his departure. The outcry against him long since had subsided. The American nation had other interests. If he returned, Theodosia suggested in her letters, people might very well take no heed of his past.

In March, 1812, Burr completed his arrangements. Wearing a black wig and whiskers to disguise himself, he boarded the small translantic sailing vessel *Aurora* and sailed from England for the United States. Five weeks later, when he arrived in Boston, no one greeted him. Theodosia and her family were in South Carolina; no one else knew of his return.

He remained in a friend's house in Boston for more than a week. One day a Boston newspaper reported that "Colonel Burr . . . once so celebrated for his talents and latterly so much talked of for his sufferings, arrived . . . from France and England . . . on his way to New York."

Word of his return stirred little interest, and Burr judged it safe to continue his journey. Still in disguise, he slipped aboard another ship, the *Rose,* and sailed down the coast to New York.

Not long afterward a New York newspaper stated that "Aaron Burr has returned to the city, and has resumed the practice of law. . . ."

A little tin sign above the door at 9 Nassau Street proclaimed the fact that Aaron Burr had indeed returned and reopened his law office. The idle and curious came by and stared. There was no alarm, no violent stir. A few old friends visited him hesitantly. Prospective clients came, too, for Burr's great reputation as a lawyer had not been forgotten. The first week at Nassau Street he earned $2,000. But at once old creditors began to emerge. Though Burr was to practice law for the rest of his life, his debts were so great that he never would be free of them.

Burr was now fifty-six, and his principal desire was to be reunited with his daughter and grandson. He lived entirely for them. He urged Theodosia to bring Gamp north for a visit.

In a single postal delivery from the South he received two replies. The first, from Theodosia, said:

A few miserable days past, my dear father, and your late letters would have gladdened my soul . . . but there is no more joy for me; the world is a blank. I have lost my boy. My child is gone for ever. He expired on the 30th of June. My head is not now sufficiently collected to say any thing further. May Heaven, by other blessings, make you some amends for the noble grandson you have lost.

The other letter was from Theodosia's husband, Joseph Alston:

That boy, on whom we all rested, our companion, our friend . . . he who was to have redeemed all your glory, and shed new luster on our families—that boy, at once our happiness and our pride is taken from us—is dead.

There was only one person left to him in the world. Burr wrote Theodosia, whom he had not seen in almost five years, urging her to come north. She replied that she would.

Her ship, the *Patriot*, sailed from Charleston on December 30, 1812. A British warship reported sighting the vessel off Cape Hatteras. After that, the *Patriot* was not seen again.

Burr waited as the days and weeks went by. The overdue ship carried all his hopes. He haunted the Battery at the tip of Manhattan, his eyes fixed on the harbor entrance. But the sails of the *Patriot* never appeared.

With the death of Theodosia and Gamp, Burr's ambitions were finally extinguished. There were no more plots or plans, no more dreams of glory. He was like a volcano become suddenly extinct; outwardly unchanged, there no longer was any heat or fire within.

For almost a quarter of a century Burr lived quietly in New York. His existence was empty, without real purpose, without warm family ties. For diversion, he read the latest books of philosophy and history; he practiced law—and, as always, had unpaid debts.

At the age of seventy-seven, he remarried. His bride was almost twenty years younger, the last of literally hundreds of women he had charmed. But Burr's interest in the Widow Jumel was not entirely romantic. She was very rich, and within six months of their wedding they quarreled over his spending habits. Then they parted and she sued for divorce, claiming that he had thrown away a considerable portion of her property and would have spent the rest in a short time if she had not left him. Apparently, to the very end, Burr was as improvident as ever.

He died on September 14, 1836, at Staten Island, New York, just a few miles across the water from his boyhood home at Elizabethtown. A half-dozen old friends served as pallbearers, carrying the coffin of a man whose extraordinary gifts had promised so much, yet had achieved so little.

He was buried in the college chapel cemetery at Princeton in an unmarked grave.

Bibliogrpahy

Abernethy, Thomas P., *The Burr Conspiracy*. Oxford University Press, 1954.

Chesterton, Cecil, *A History of the United States*. E. P. Dutton Co., New York.

Davis, Matthew L. (Ed.), *The Private Journals of Aaron Burr*. Harper and Bros., 1838.

Jones, Phyllis M. (Ed.), *Letters of Lord Chesterfield*. Oxford University Press.

Lucas, F. L., *The Search for Good Sense*. The Macmillan Co., 1961.

Miller, William, *A History of the United States*. Dell Publishing Company, New York.

Morison, Samuel E., *The Oxford History of the American People*. Oxford University Press, 1965.

Nye, R. B., and Morpurgo, J. E., *A History of the United States*. Penguin Books Inc., Baltimore.

Parton, James, *The Life and Times of Aaron Burr*. Mason Bros., 1861.

Schachner, Nathan, *Aaron Burr*. A. S. Barnes & Co., 1961.

Schachner, Nathan, *Alexander Hamilton.* Thomas Yoseloff Inc., New York, 1957.

Scheer, George F., and Rankin, Hugh F. (Eds.), *Rebels and Redcoats.* New American Library.

The Encyclopaedia Britannica, 1964.

Dictionary of American Biography. Scribners, 1929.

The Columbia Encyclopaedia.

Index

189

The Author

In *Aaron Burr* William Wise has written a biography to compare with his widely read *Alexander Hamilton,* a Junior Literary Guild selection that has been reprinted extensively by the United States Information Service. Mr. Wise, who attended Yale and served with the U.S. Army in Europe during World War II, has written many books for readers of all ages. For his *The Two Reigns of Tutankhamen* he received a Boys' Clubs of America Junior Book Award Medal. He lives in his native New York.